The Essential Bible Companion to the Psalms

ESSENTIAL BIBLE COMPANION SERIES

The Essential Bible Companion to the Psalms

Key Insights for Reading God's Word

Brian L. Webster and David R. Beach

ZONDERVAN®

ZONDERVAN.com/
AUTHORTRACKER
follow your favorite authors

ZONDERVAN

The Essential Bible Companion to the Psalms

This title is also available as a Zondervan ebook.
Visit www.zondervan.com/ebooks.

This title is also available in a Zondervan audio edition.
Visit www.zondervan.fm.

Requests for information should be addressed to:

Zondervan, *Grand Rapids, Michigan 49530*

Library of Congress Cataloging-in-Publication Data

Webster, Brian L., 1965-
The essential Bible companion to the Psalms : key insights for reading God's Word /
Brian L. Webster and David R. Beach.
p. cm.
ISBN 978-0-310-28689-9 (softcover)
1. Bible. O.T. Psalms—Criticism, interpretation, etc. I. Beach, David R., 8/30/1956- II. Title.
BS1430.52.W43 2010
223'.2061—dc22 2009046399

Cover photography: Steve Gardner, Pixelworks Studio; Z. Radovan/www.BibleLandPictures.com
Interior design: Mark Sheeres

Printed in China

11 12 13 14 15 16 /CTC/ 23 22 21 20 19 18 17 16 15 14 13 12 11 10 9 8 7 6 5 4 3 2

Contents

Acknowledgments

I would like to thank my former Psalms professors, Dr. John Stek (Calvin Theological Seminary) and Dr. Alan Cooper (Hebrew Union College, now at Jewish Theological Seminary). I am particularly indebted to Dr. Stek for allowing me to review his structural layouts as I continue to work on the Psalms for a commentary in Zondervan's forthcoming series Hearing the Message of Scripture.

While this book was in publication, Dr. Stek went home to be with his Lord. I would like to dedicate this work to his memory.

The Rev. Dr. John Stek was a great scholar, teacher, and churchman, gracious and dedicated to helping the common person understand God's Word. He was a leader among Bible translators. He served for decades on the translation committee for the NIV, including being Chair of the Committee on Bible Translation; was an associate editor of the TNIV Study Bible; and worked also on the NIV Study Bible and TNIV Study Bible. He imparted to his students a love for the beauty of Hebrew poetry, and we remain in his debt. May this volume be an honor to his legacy.

I am grateful to Dave Beach for many fruitful discussions about faith in relationships, lament, and the Psalms.

Thanks to David Frees and the rest of the Zondervan team for the opportunity and for the professional care given to this project.

Thanks to my parents, Allen and Lynn Webster, for their essential support throughout the years.

And finally, thanks to my wife and daughters, Hope, Angela, Lily, Robyn, and Starla, for their love and encouragement.

Brian Webster

I would like to acknowledge all of those who have impacted my life with a love for God, for his Word, and for my neighbor. Space, however, limits me to listing those most notable. In chronological order:

First, my parents, Richard and Eileen Beach, whose unwavering fidelity to God's Word accompanied me in the beginning of my journey. I bless you.

Second, my loving and ever lovely wife, Cynthia, who constantly encourages me and blesses me with her words and a smile. You are the full expression of love to me. I love and bless you.

Third, Brian Webster, who first as my Greek professor and then as my friend has invited me, encouraged me, and inspired me to write my heart on matters of the heart in the Psalms. I bless you.

Fourth, Dan Allender and Tremper Longman, whose friendship and commitment to each other allowed them the pleasure of writing together *Cry of the Soul*, a book that more than any other has birthed and coached my desire to write with Brian our words on the Psalms. I bless and thank you.

Additionally, there are others who wait on the other side—my brother Dick; my first wife, Sue; my grandparents; and others I have known—cheering me on this journey into Christ.

Last, the team at Zondervan, whose invitation and welcome have meant more to me than they will ever know. May God expand your territories for his kingdom and his people.

David R. Beach

INTRODUCTION TO THE PSALMS

Overview

The Psalms. Their hymns lead us in praising God. Their laments unleash our cries for help. Their royal ceremonies and songs of Zion assert God's order. Still other psalms lead us to reflect on God's Word or call us to righteous character.

The Psalms may be the most read book of the Old Testament and are well loved for many reasons. We can enter into a multitude of varied scenes painted by poetic brushstrokes on its verbal canvas because their substance resonates with our lives and experiences. They may be scenes of rejoicing, despair, confident hope, uncertainty, or solemn moments of profound musings. Here or there, for a time as needed, we can enter and sit with the psalmists, then join our voices across the ages with poets whose words become our expressions. They become our words of praise or of disappointment with God or our cries for justice or mercy. And as the psalmist's words embody our feelings and sentiments, they also lead us to a better understanding of God and a deeper encounter with him. Whether we would sing with abandon or cry out feeling abandoned, the Psalms are faithful companions, and we do well to visit them often.

While we feel welcome visiting with the psalmists, we are sometimes well aware that we are visitors. They speak of geography that we have not visited, countries no longer on the map, and weapons from the wars of days gone by. We live with different political structures and social institutions. Certain turns of phrase are understandable but have a foreign ring. Nevertheless, the Psalms still speak powerfully to us with a timeless essence and an open invitation.

Our hope is for this volume to be an unobtrusive yet vital companion as you read the Psalms. While we do not aim to explain every poetic line, we do hope to help you select where to visit and to provide a basic orientation as you read each psalm. We point out essential elements and shed light on occasional phrases or identify relevant information about the setting.

In This Book

Following the introduction, we present the following information on the Psalms as an aid to reading them in your Bible.

THEME: States the main idea of the psalm

TYPE: Classifies the psalm by its literary type, such as lament by an individual, hymn of thanksgiving, praise, royal, etc.

AUTHOR: Supplies information about the author, musical notations, and historical notes

BACKGROUND: Elaborates on the historical or theological background of the psalm and its connections to other biblical passages

STRUCTURE: Describes how the lines of poetry are grouped into stanzas and gives a basic sketch of the flow of thought

SPECIAL NOTES: Makes miscellaneous comments on words or phrases in the psalm

REFLECTION: Applies the concepts or images in the psalm and their significance for us today

Following is an explanation of the categories mentioned above, as well as a general orientation to the book of Psalms and its poetry.

Perspectives on the Psalter

The Psalms as Songs

The original Hebrew title of the book, Tehillim (pronounced te-hil-léem), labels the Psalms as "praises," and truly they are to be sung. David is known for playing the harp, and the Psalms refer to several more instruments: lyre, lute, trumpet, timbrel, horn, and cymbals. These would not have been like the modern instruments of the same name, but they are clearly used to accompany the singing of the Psalms in public worship: "come before him with joyful songs" (100:2); "praise him with timbrel and dancing" (150:4).

The Psalms were sung on general occasions of public assembly for worship, including the specific occasions of religious festivals, such as Passover. But they were also sung as pilgrims traveled to Jerusalem to worship. It is natural to assume that families did not limit singing such psalms to the actual festival day, but would learn and practice them in other settings, such as at home and in private as preparation and personal expression. Yes, they were for public worship, but not exclusively so. They were—and still are today—great teaching tools and good memory aids that brought a message to mind.

For example, Moses taught the people a song (Deut. 32) as a teaching tool in light of their tendency to rebel (31:19). It recalled God's acts, pointed out his character, reminded Israel of their intended relationship with God, condemned their rebellion, proclaimed judgment, and forecasted restoration. It was to be performed in public and sung by the community. But it was also intended for continued reflection by families and individuals. Public singing is important for the purpose of worship, but its prominent place in community life serves as strong affirmation that songs can also be integral in teaching the community.

The Psalms as Ceremony

Many psalms may have been sung by a choir or the congregation as if they were one voice—a simple presentation. Others reflect ceremonies with more than one speaker. They may have been for religious holidays or royal ceremonies, or they may incorporate a priestly or prophetic voice speaking to the community (cf. Pss. 20, 62, 91). Thus a psalm may shift from addressing God to addressing the people or an individual; from speaking as "we" to speaking as "I"; from speaking to God, to God speaking. Such psalms remind us that we are not alone in the walk of faith; we are not the only voice. Rather, we are in community and in relationship with God.

The Psalms as Prayers

Psalm 72 is followed by the closing remark, "This concludes the prayers of David son of Jesse." Clearly, not all of the Psalms are for worship or ceremonies. Many psalms are cries to God for help and deliverance. They are prayers set in the form of poetry. They are personal, filled with the anxieties of real hardships, but often stated in generalized terms so that others can say the same words while reflecting on their own personal crises.

Sometimes the prayers reflect the specific concerns of the Davidic king. In these cases people were called into community, to enter the prayer as loyal subjects of the Lord's anointed. The community shared common enemies and other concerns with the king and was concerned for the king, having a stake in his fortunes before God. For as God deals with his anointed, all his followers are affected. The king's prayers serve as models for how the rest of the community may approach God, as indeed, the king himself was to be a role model for the people in obeying and worshiping God. Thus, while at times subjects need to respect the difference between themselves and the king, they are also invited into these psalms.

The Psalms as Book

The Psalms come to us today in the form of a book made up of five smaller books (Pss. 1–41, 42–72, 73–89, 90–106, and 107–150). It does not have a musical score and does not begin with a hymn or a prayer. Psalm 1 acts as an introduction to the whole book. In addition, the beginning and ending psalm of each of the five books are often considered key thematic transitions. While it would be making too much of the organization of the Psalter to try to find a tight connection between each psalm and its neighboring psalms, they are no longer isolated songs, but a collection of poems comprising a book for contemplation.

This book of five books has songs, ceremonies, and prayers. So sing them, perform them, pray them, and study them. You will never reach their depths or come up dry.

Groups of Psalms in the Psalter

Several characteristics suggest connecting certain psalms into groups. The Psalter is divided into five books, which is a clear set of groups. Others share the same author, such as Asaph or the Sons of Korah. Still others are of a similar type; that is, they have common internal characteristics regardless of author or place in the Psalter, for example, laments. Our presentation of the Psalms classifies them according to the types explained below. We also describe each Psalm's structure, referring to the communication roles of the units of each psalm. (See the quick reference chart Common Elements of the Psalms.)

Types of Psalms

The Psalms are grouped into different types, called genres, based on the kinds of things they say, the emotional mood they invoke, and how they depict certain speakers, such as the whole community, or an individual, or perhaps the king. The main types include praise hymns, laments, psalms that instruct, those specifically for liturgical use, and those for the king. We can divide these types into smaller categories. But at some point we realize these are artificial categories, because the ancient poets could and did write creatively. They might omit or add to the "normal" elements, rearrange the sequences of parts, mix two "types," or cross the general "boundaries" that we see now. Nonetheless, collecting them in certain groups is helpful, because it allows us to see common elements, trends, and meaningful variations.

Hymns

When we call certain psalms hymns, we do not mean the same sort of songs that one finds in a hymnal. The hymnal evokes a certain kind of musical style and contains songs that usually have several verses plus a chorus that repeats. The word *hymn* means a song of praise. Psalms that are hymns of praise can vary in their poetic design and be sung as a community "we" or an individual "I," but their basic content is to praise God. The hymns can be divided into groups: hymns of praise, hymns of thanksgiving, hymns of the Lord's kingship, and Zion songs.

Hymns of Praise

The generic category of hymn includes various types of hymns that have additional characteristics in the way they offer praise. Hymns of praise may include three main communication tasks: *calls to praise*, *motivation to praise*, and *praise itself*. Calls to praise invite or instruct others to give praise to the Lord. Motivation to praise means the psalmist provides reasons or motives to give praise to the Lord. Besides variation in construction, the hymns can emphasize these three aspects in different amounts. For example, some hymns of praise are exclusively calls to praise.

Hymns of Thanksgiving

Even though the English word "thank" appears frequently in Bible translations, Hebrew does not actually have a word that means to thank. The word usually translated "thank" means something more like "praise," "confess," or "give credit to." The distinguishing feature of the hymns of thanksgiving is that they give credit to God for what he has done in someone's life. While a generic hymn of praise might emphasize describing God's awesome characteristics, the person singing the hymn of thanksgiving has a story to tell or a report to make on how God acted in his or her life. Hymns of thanksgiving are often subdivided into individual thanksgiving and communal thanksgiving, depending on whether the speaker is a first person singular "I" or plural "we." Some psalms have both, which typically means there were roles for a leader as well as for the assembled people.

Hymns of Praise/Thanksgiving

Hymns of praise or thanksgiving are psalms that have some thanksgiving elements as well as other characteristics of hymns of praise. That is, at least part of these hymns report or refer to how God should be credited for acting in the life of a person or the nation. Some may classify these psalms differently, but we have chosen to indicate the mixture in the title.

Hymns of the Lord's Kingship

Another subcategory of the hymns of praise is hymns of the Lord's kingship, also known as enthronement hymns. They celebrate in particular the Lord's kingship and tend to use the phrase "the LORD reigns" to refer to his throne and tell of the establishment or extent of his rule.

Hymns: Zion Songs

The title "Zion songs" comes from Psalm 137:3. Songs of Zion are hymns of praise that emphasize the location of Zion, another name for Jerusalem. King David made Jerusalem his capital, and the Lord chose it (cf. Deut. 12:3–28) as the place for the temple that was built under David's son, King Solomon. The temple, and especially the ark of the covenant, symbolized God's presence on earth. (The ark of the covenant had been made under Moses' leadership and was normally kept in the tabernacle from the time it was built after Israel received the Law at Mount Sinai until the temple was built.) The Lord lives and reigns in heaven and rules over all the earth, but Jerusalem is seen as a special place of connection between his heavenly and earthly sovereignty. Since many psalms mention Zion, classifying them as Zion songs is partly a judgment call in light of how much Jerusalem is emphasized as well as whether they are hymns of praise.

Laments/Cries for Help: Individual or Communal

The most common type of psalm is the lament. Sometimes called complaint psalms, the essential element is the cry for help during distress. The English terms *lament* and *grief* can refer to mourning in connection with a death, but they are not exclusively tied to mourning and funerals. When describing psalms, the term *lament* is used in the broader sense of an expression of sorrow, grief, or disappointment. Lament psalms tell of a person's or community's lamenting in their distress as they turn to God for help. This kind of complaint is not like the grumbling and complaining of Israel in the wilderness. There they complained against God while speaking to each other with bad attitudes. In the laments the psalmists complain of their situation. And though freely expressing their disappointment with God, they are turning *to* him, not away.

The components of lament psalms may perform several communication roles: initial appeal to be heard, lament over distress, accusation against enemies, complaint against God, claim of innocence or loyalty, confession of sin, petition, imprecation, motivation to answer, statement of confidence, and vow to praise God. A lament psalm does not necessarily have all of these elements, and their order may vary. But these labels (briefly described in the quick reference charts) provide a helpful way to track the general flow of thought. In addition, two perennial questions permeate the lament psalms: "Why?" and "How long?" Why is this happening? How long will it last? Typically these questions occur in the lament, accusation, or complaint sections. They emphasize the distress and angst that characterize this category of psalm.

Psalms of Confidence

Because psalms of lament typically have a statement of confidence, psalms of confidence are often considered to have developed from laments into a category of their own. They may still have brief elements of petition, reference to difficulties or enemies, or affirmations of loyalty, but in the main they speak of confidence in the Lord's care and protection (cf. Ps. 23). They may sound similar to a hymn of thanksgiving, but the hymn of thanksgiving tells of a story from the past while the hymn of confidence projects into the future.

Royal Psalms

A royal psalm is one that involves the king and may also belong to another category. That is, the king may be the speaker in a lament psalm or hymn of praise or thanksgiving. But some psalms have an exclusively royal nature, perhaps being about the coronation of the king, God's covenant with the line of David, or the royal wedding, or being a prayer for the king made by the community. These latter kinds of psalms are classified only as royal psalms. Sometimes it is difficult to be certain whether the king is an intended speaker in a given psalm; therefore not everyone is in agreement about how many psalms involve the king. Often the list is limited to those that specifically mention "king," "anointed," or "David." Ours is expanded, and additionally we list several psalms as possibly royal. Being a royal psalm is also not simply a matter of authorship. A psalm may be ascribed to David but be from a time while Saul was still king and be preserved as an example for how anyone might pray in similar circumstances.

Liturgy Psalms

When describing liturgy psalms, *liturgy* does not mean the order of a religious service or simply use in a service. A hymn that is basically a call to praise may have appeared in a service prior to hymns of praise or testimonies of thanksgiving made by the worshipers. In fact, several types may have appeared in the order of a service, so if use in a service were the only criteria, we would probably have to classify all 150 psalms as liturgical. Instead, the key characteristic behind this label is that the psalm contains roles for different speakers. Several speakers, or speaking voices, appear in the Psalter: individuals, such as the king, a priest or prophet, the common worshiper, enemies, or even God, and also groups, such as the assembled community, people approaching or leaving Jerusalem, priests, or the gatekeepers.

Some psalms have a deliberate interplay between two or more of these voices. But, for example, the recitation of the enemies' words are not liturgical. However, when a psalm envisions multiple parties in its performance for a service or invites the meditative reader to view it so, we call it liturgical.

Instructional and Wisdom Psalms

Most often the psalmists address God, crying out for help or responding in praise. Sometimes they address people, such as making a call to the community to praise God, or the priest and people address each other. Beyond these exchanges, quite a few psalms have at least a section in which they instruct. The teaching may or may not be like a prophetic word and may address the king, the people, or even foreigners. These teaching portions are most often embedded in psalms classified as other types. Therefore most of the psalms that are called "mixed" in type are in part instructional. A smaller number have some more specific characteristics like proverbs and other wisdom literature in the Bible. These are often called wisdom psalms.

Collections and Arrangements in the Psalter

Superscriptions

Classifying the Psalms according to their type, or genre, helps us get a handle on several things, but these are our modern labels. Most of the 150 psalms come with their own headings, called superscriptions. These may contain references to persons, historical information, classifications, or musical aspects. They can also be used to place the Psalms into groups. Unfortunately, the meaning of much of the material in the superscriptions is not as clear to us as we would like. One result is that many Bible translations simply take some of the Hebrew words and spell them with English letters, such as *miktam* (Pss. 16, 56–60). The unfamiliar Hebrew words and the uncertainty of some of their meanings will make this section seem a bit more technical than the rest of the introduction. A list of unusual terms in the Psalter appears at the end of this section with pronunciation guides and possible meanings (see page 29).

Persons

The people in the superscriptions include the position of "director" and several people mentioned by name: David, Asaph, the Sons of Korah, Moses, Solomon, Ethan, and Heman. The term "director" or "leader" comes from the Hebrew *menatstseah* (meh-nahts-tsay-akh). The phrase "for the director" occurs in fifty-five superscriptions, all but once as the first word. Every occurrence is in a psalm of David, Asaph, or the Sons of Korah. Furthermore, these are the only psalms that mention other musical aspects. This person seems to be some kind of "director of music" (NIV), such as a "choir director" (NASB) or possibly a master of ceremonies, though some have wondered whether the "leader" could relate to a role for the king or other official.

At first glance, the personal names mentioned in the superscriptions appear to be authors. But the personal names are preceded by the same Hebrew preposition as the "director," and in one psalm more than one name is mentioned (Ps. 88 mentions the Sons of Korah and Heman). This preposition (Heb., *le*) could mean "by," "for," or "about." So if the Psalm is "*le* David," it could mean it is written *by* David, written or collected *for* David, or written *about* David or the Davidic line. And quite possibly it does not mean the same thing in each case. Some may be by David while others are for or about David or the reigning king of the Davidic dynasty. (Both the Dead

Sea Scrolls' copies of the Psalms and the ancient Greek translation, the Septuagint, position "*le* David" in front of more Psalms than our Bibles, which may indicate that scribes had been adding this title to Psalms for their own purposes.)

Of the people named in the superscriptions, David, Solomon, and Moses are well known, as is David's reputation as a musician and songwriter. The lesser-known names go back to appointments made by David. The Sons of Korah reach back to the time of Moses. Korah led a rebellion (Num. 16) and was swallowed up in an earthquake, but his sons survived (Num. 26:11). They and their descendents served as Levites. They supported David during the time of Saul (1 Chron. 12:6), and David appointed them as gatekeepers for the temple (1 Chron. 26:19), a position they resumed after the exile (1 Chron. 9:19). David also appointed Asaph, a seer who prophesied, as chief musician (1 Chron. 16:5, 7, 37; 25:2; 2 Chron. 29:30; Neh. 12:46) and appointed others, including Heman and Ethan (1 Chron. 15:19). The descendants of Asaph also resumed their duties after the exile (Ezra 2:41).

Historical Information

Historical information always occurs last in the superscriptions and appears only in psalms of David. Thirteen superscriptions contain historical information (Pss. 3, 7, 18, 34, 51, 52, 54, 56, 57, 59, 60, 63, 142). It is not certain whether these parts of the superscriptions were all penned by David, were traditions preserved by the priests and written later, or were simply interpretive suggestions made by scribes for understanding the psalms in light of the accounts in 1 and 2 Samuel.

Additionally, some psalms refer to occasions though not to the historical circumstances of David's life. Psalm 30 is for the "dedication of the house" (TNIV, "temple"), which might refer to the temple or palace. Psalm 45 is a "wedding song" for the king. Psalm 92 is "For the Sabbath day." Psalm 100 is "For giving grateful praise." And Psalm 102 is "A prayer of an afflicted man. When he is faint and pours out his lament before the Lord" (NIV).

Classifications

The meaning of the classifications is not always clear, so the translations often use the Hebrew words instead of a translation. The three most common classifications are (1) *mizmor,* "psalm"; (2) *shir,* "song"; and (3) *maskil,* which seems to mean for skilled playing or for giving understanding (since the root of the word relates to skill or understanding). A special category of "songs" is the "Songs of Ascents," Psalms 120–134. The exact difference between a "psalm" and a "song" is not completely certain, and some psalms are classified as both. Possibly the title "psalm" (*mizmor*) refers to instrumentation and "song" (*shir*) refers to a vocal element, which would explain why both can be applied to the same composition. Both "psalm" (*mizmor*) and "song" (*shir*) appear in psalms that are laments as well as hymns and other types. *Maskil* also appears as the heading in several types of psalms, though it has not been applied to any hymns of praise.

A few psalms are labeled as a "prayer" (*tephillah*), "praise" (*tehillah*), *miktam,* or *shiggaion* (shig-guy-own), the meaning of the latter two being quite unclear. The five psalms labeled as a "prayer" (Pss. 17, 86, 90, 102, 142) are all laments including petition, while the single psalm labeled "praise" (*tehillah,* Ps. 145), is a hymn of praise. The application of the titles to these psalms is not surprising, but since most laments and hymns are not labeled this way, the reason for their use in these cases is not clear. The root of the word *miktam* may relate this title to the idea of covering or being overwhelmed. But even if this is so, how it applies to these psalms can be imagined in many ways, leaving us in the dark. We can observe, however, that these psalms (Ps. 16, a psalm of confidence, and

Pss. 56–60, all laments) concern dire circumstances. Psalm 7 is the only *shiggaion*, a variant of which also occurs in Habakkuk 3:1. Based on its root, the term might have to do with "wandering," which we could imagine musically as a tune that employs a wide range of notes (wandering up and down the scale). *Shiggaion* has also been connected with the idea of "fervor" or "passionate lament." But these are only guesses; no one really knows.

Musical Aspects

Musical aspects occur only in superscriptions that also say, "For the director of music." Psalms 4, 6, 54, 55, 61, 67, and 76 are said to be accompanied "with" or played "on" stringed instruments (called *neginoth*, neh-gee-note) and Psalm 5 on a wind instrument (*nechilot*, neh-khee-lote, often translated "flute"). Possibly Psalms 6 and 12 refer to an eight-stringed instrument, a type of lyre (*sheminith*, sheh-mee-neet). A few psalms may refer to instrument tunings, either for male voices (Pss. 6 and 12, another understanding of *sheminith*) or for female voices (Ps. 46, which is *al-alamoth*, and Ps. 9, which is *almut labben*, though this is understood as a tune in the NIV).

Some of the material in the superscriptions may refer to musical styles, perhaps from different cities or regions in the Near East. Examples include Psalms 8, 81, 84 (*gittith*, git-teet), Psalms 39, 62, 77 (*jeduthun*, yeh-doo-toon), Psalm 53 (*mahalath*, mah-khah-lot), and Psalm 88 (*mahalath leannoth*, mah-khah-lot leh-an-note). Two of the terms above, *sheminith* and *alamoth/almut* should be included in this possibility. The same is true for superscriptions translated as "according to the tune of." The phrase "the tune of" is not in the Hebrew but is sometimes supplied as a guess for understanding the phrases that follow, such as "Lilies" (Pss. 45, 69), "Lily of the Covenant" (Ps. 60), or "The Doe of the Morning" (Ps. 22), but the texts of these phrases are all questionable (see also Pss. 9, 56–59, 75, 80).

Collections

Leaving aside the many psalms of David, there are four main subcollections within the Psalter: psalms of Asaph, psalms of the Sons of Korah, songs of ascents, and hallelujah psalms.

Psalms of Asaph

The psalms labeled "of Asaph" (Pss. 50, 73–83) might also have been composed or collected by his descendants. Thematically they devote a good deal of thought to issues of God's justice both within Israel and in how Israel and the nations relate. Stylistically, these psalms show a preference for referring to God by the name, or rather title, Elohim, instead of by his name, Yahweh (formerly misunderstood as Jehovah). The Asaphite psalms include several instances of a prophetic or divine voice, an emphasis on history, and references to the covenant.

Psalms of the Sons of Korah

The two Korahite collections, Psalms 42–49 and 84–88 (except 86), include variety, whether measured by the ancient classifications or by the labels of modern types. They take us to the highest levels of confidence in several Zion songs and to the lowest points of discouragement in perhaps the two darkest laments of the Psalter: Psalm 44, a communal lament, and Psalm 88, an individual lament. The Sons of Korah also give us the only wedding song in the Psalter. The first collection of Korahite psalms is like those of Asaph in favoring the title Elohim when referring to God; however, the second collection favors using the divine name Yahweh.

Songs of Ascents

Fifteen psalms, 120–134, are labeled "A Song of Ascents." These songs include individual and communal laments, psalms of confidence, Zion songs, wisdom psalms, royal psalms, and psalms of mixed type. But the heavy emphasis on Jerusalem throughout this section, combined with other factors, has brought the greatest support for the idea that these were psalms sung when going on a pilgrimage to Jerusalem. Psalm 122 explicitly talks of pilgrimage (cf. Ex. 24:13; 34:23; Lev. 23:4–8; and Deut. 16 on religious journeys to Jerusalem). The central psalm of this group, Psalm 127, has been associated with Solomon for its mention of the "house," taken to mean the temple. A number have harvest imagery, which suggests the Feast of Tabernacles. And later Jewish tradition suggests that the Levites, at some point after the return from exile, sang these fifteen psalms during the Feast of Tabernacles as they went up the fifteen steps between the outer courts of the temple. This does not mean that they were originally composed as one group or that they were the only psalms ever sung on a pilgrimage, but that they became associated over time, and tradition grouped them together.

Hallelujah Psalms

Fifteen psalms either begin or end, or do both, with the Hebrew imperative *halleluyah*, "Praise the LORD." Psalm 114 is usually included with these because of its character and in part on the possibility that the halleluyah closing Psalm 113 belongs with Psalm 114. They mostly fall into three groups, Psalms 104–106, 111–117, and 146–150, but also 135. Each is anonymous, lacking any superscription. In general they are hymns of praise or thanksgiving, though occasionally of mixed type. The two groups Psalms 104–106 and 146–150 end the fourth and fifth books of the Psalter.

The Five Books

The first two psalms of book 1 of the Psalter, Psalms 1–41, are introductory. Psalm 1 is a wisdom psalm. It advocates the study of God's law and meditation on his Word. This encourages us to treat the Psalter as a book for study and contemplation. Psalm 2 is royal and celebrates the Lord's rule through the king in Jerusalem. It may have been used each time a new king was crowned. Thus it introduces us to the Psalter with royal concerns, which are visited again at key points in the book. Psalm 2 was probably placed as the introduction to book 1, while Psalm 1 was placed as an introduction to the whole Psalter. Yet the blessings beginning Psalm 1 and concluding Psalm 2 act as brackets around them, encouraging us to read them together.

After the anonymous Psalms 1 and 2, nearly all the psalms in book 1 are "of David." The exceptions are Psalms 10 and 33, which have no superscription. Psalm 10 is actually part of Psalm 9. Psalm 33 begins very similarly to the end of Psalm 32, which probably accounts for it being placed there. But in the main, book 1 is a collection of Davidic psalms following a royal psalm. Book 1 has several more royal psalms, several instructional psalms, and twice as many laments as hymns. References to God are predominantly by his name Yahweh.

Book 2 consists primarily of psalms of the Sons of Korah and those of David. The Korahite psalms, 42–49, are separated from the Davidic psalms by one of Asaph, 50. Psalms 51–71 are mostly of David. Psalms 66 and 67 are anonymous but have superscriptions, while Psalm 71 has no superscription and may belong as part of Psalm 70. Psalm 72 is associated with Solomon. As a royal psalm it is like a bookend with Psalm 2 on the other side. The general lack of literacy and emphasis on psalms of/for David may mean that the first two books were originally meant first for a royal readership. The title Elohim is far more common than God's name in Psalms 42–71 (Elohim 183; Yahweh 31). But like book 1, there are about twice as many laments as hymns, and the number of royal and instructional psalms is about the same as the number of hymns.

The seventeen psalms of book 3 are mainly psalms of Asaph (Pss. 73–83) and of the Sons of Korah (Pss. 84–85, 87–88), together with one of David (Ps. 86) and one of Ethan (Ps. 89). The psalms of Asaph continue in the pattern of Psalms 42–71, preferring the title Elohim over the name Yahweh (43 to 13), while the rest of book 3, including the second section of the sons of Korah, prefers the name Yahweh (31 to 16). Book 3 ends with a royal psalm, as does book 2, though not with such a positive outlook for the kingship. Again the number of laments is about double that of hymns, while the number of royal psalms is similar to the number of hymns, but there is a higher number of instructional psalms.

The seventeen psalms of book 4, Psalms 90–106, are mostly anonymous, but with one associated with Moses (90) and two with David (101, 103). The Lord's name, Yahweh, predominates over Elohim when referring to God (105 to 24). But now hymns outnumber laments three to one (13 to 4), and there are about the same number of royal and instructional psalms as laments. Three hallelujah psalms end book 4.

Book 5, Psalms 107–150, is again mostly anonymous but includes fifteen of David and one of Solomon. Issues raised at the end of book 4 in Psalm 106 are addressed in Psalm 107, which is followed by three psalms of David. Next are a series of hallelujah psalms (Pss. 111–117), leading to a liturgy (Ps. 118) and the unique Psalm 119, emphasizing God's law. Psalms 120–134 are psalms of ascents. The first seven and the last seven, 120–126 and 128–134, each use the Lord's name twenty-four times and include two psalms of David, while the center psalm of the group is of Solomon. Following three psalms without superscriptions are seven more of David (Pss. 138–145). A series of five hallelujah psalms (Pss. 146–150) close the book. Book 5 again favors use of the Lord's name Yahweh over Elohim (236 to 31). Like book 4, it has more hymns than laments (23 to 13). It also has a handful of royal psalms and a couple handfuls of instructional psalms.

When we look back on the whole Psalter, we can see a loose amount of organization based on names of "authors" and names of God. Royal psalms stand at key points in the first three books. And laments diminish after book 3 in favor of hymns in the fourth and fifth books. Each of the five books ends with a doxology (cf. Pss. 41:13; 72:18–19; 89:52; 106:48; 150:6), though the series of hallelujah psalms ending book 5 magnifies this far more than the previous books. Some people also see an emphasis on eschatological hope in the broad sweep of the progression of the Psalms.

The Poetry of the Psalms

We talk about stanzas and poetic lines, but the lines do not rhyme, and the stanzas are not like those of modern hymns. The Hebrew poetry of the Bible is not like English poetry. Instead of thinking of poetic lines that have rhyming words at the end, a line of poetry from the Psalms usually has two or three main segments. This is why many Bible translations use indentations in lines of poetry. The first segment starts at the edge of the margin; following segments are slightly indented. Because the segments often are wider than the margins, the segments have to wrap around, resulting in more indentation to keep each segment together and distinct from the others. With so much indentation, it can be easy to lose track. Plus it is not as simple as following the verse numbers, because the verse numbers do not necessarily match the poetic lines. Sometimes a Bible verse will have more than one poetic line, and sometimes only part of one.

A Hebrew poetic line often has more than one segment (and may be called a monocolon, bicolon, or tricolon, depending on whether it has one, two, or three parts). The parts are usually brief and of similar length in Hebrew, though English does not represent this well. Instead of rhyming, the parts of the line have a quality called parallelism; the parts work together as sets to convey their main idea. They may work together with the second line restating the same idea (synonymous parallelism, e.g., Ps. 19:1), giving its opposite (antithetic parallelism, e.g., Ps. 75:10), or completing the thought begun in the previous line (synthetic parallelism, e.g., Ps. 119:11).

Synonymous parallelism: Psalm 19:1

The heavens declare the glory of God;
the skies proclaim the work of his hands.

Antithetic parallelism: Psalm 75:10

I will cut off the horns of all the wicked,
but the horns of the righteous will be lifted up.

Synthetic parallelism: Psalm 119:11

I have hidden your word in my heart
that I might not sin against you.

When several lines form a group with a similar purpose, we call that a stanza, but this is a different use of the term than the arrangement of stanzas in a modern hymn. Because of these characteristics, a good reading strategy is to treat each poetic line, bicolon or tricolon, as a package and reflect on how the parts work together to say an idea and give it nuances. Then proceed to the stanzas and consider how the lines make up a big picture. Next observe how the flow of thought goes from the picture in one stanza to the next. The goal of the Structure sections in the entries on the Psalms in part 3 is to assist with identifying the stanzas and how their big ideas connect together.

The psalmists are usually very deliberate about the structure of their compositions. Perhaps this is most obvious with alphabetic acrostics, in which each line starts with a successive letter of the Hebrew alphabet. But it is also reflected in symmetries and patterns in the length and arrangement of the stanzas. For example, Psalm 147 has five stanzas. The first, third, and fifth have two lines, while the second and fourth each have seven lines, making an overall pattern of 2-7-2-7-2.

Personalizing the Psalms

Personalizing the Psalms involves several conversations: with self, with Scripture, with community, and with God. By its placement, Psalm 1 advises us that being rooted in God's instruction is essential for our exploration and use of the Psalms. It praises the one who delights in and meditates on the Lord's law. "Meditating" is actually a term of speaking, which can include talking to oneself, or self-talk. The word for God's "law," *torah*, can mean instruction in a general sense or be a reference to the Books of the Law (Genesis through Deuteronomy), which were the foundation of Israel's Bible, religious thought, and worldview. At the same time, the Psalms themselves are intensely relational and conversational. They are usually addressed to God and often in the setting of the community. We drink them in most deeply in these several conversations.

When we pray a psalm, we are taking someone else's words, from someone else's situation, onto our lips for our situation. The Psalms were indeed designed for this, but beyond simply feeling attracted to certain verses, how do we go about it? When we read, sing, or pray a psalm, we enter into a conversation. We might first find verses that seem compelling, but we go on to read the whole psalm.

At this point we talk to ourselves, both to see if the psalm matches our situation and if we match up to the psalm. It is not a question of finding a precise match in circumstances. The Psalms usually use general language, precisely so that they can fit different circumstances of similar character and be reused by other worshipers. What is important is the character of the situation and of the one praying. This way of looking at the Psalms involves looking at ourselves. Does the protestation of innocence fit our life, or would confession of sin be the most appropriate? Complaint to God is inherently approved in the laments, but the whining and complaining of Israel in the books of the Law was not. Where are we? How are we directing the energy of our disappointments?

By this time, we are also in a conversation with Scripture, in this case with Torah, letting it speak to how we voice complaint, letting Scripture critique us in light of its original audience. We have self-talk—examining our lives, applying the light of Torah, and positioning ourselves in the Psalms. To own these expressions as ours, we not only shape their words with our mouths, but we must let our spirits be guided by their wisdom. So we copy the psalmists, changing out our particular situation for theirs, yet follow their lead in approaching God.

We can, then, pray the Psalms just as they are worded. In character they may fit us and we fit them very closely. But it is also appropriate to pause in reading the words of the text and add lines that are specific to our situation. The psalm might praise God or call people to praise, and we mention specific things God has done for us. Some of the ancient ceremonies invited this. Or when we lament, we might let the psalmist provide the words that we cannot form while in our pain. Or in our conversation with God, we might expand on those words by declaring our own specific afflictions, still trusting the attitude of the psalmist to shepherd us in how we speak to the Almighty.

We also see that we are in conversation with two communities, one that furnished us with prayers and one in which we pray. Accepting the guidance of the past community of faith expressed in inspired Scripture builds our world-view and understanding of relating to God. There are some things, lessons and changes from life experience, that we cannot know ahead of time. When certain events come our way, we arrive at a place where some of the historical community has already been—and has left us words. Some in our current community have been to such places as well. Our nearness to our reasons to give thanks or our causes to lament may give different levels of strength and intensity to our voices in different parts of a psalm. We need to hear the call of others to praise and be part of a community when we lament. We benefit from hearing the voices of others speak the words of the psalms we need to pray.

We are also fundamentally in conversation with God. The Lord is King, who reigns and is worthy of all praise. We position ourselves before him properly as worshipers. But we also lament, in impassioned expressions not content with the status quo. Unwilling to process pain without God, we presume upon his intervention. The Psalms are about pursuing authentic relationship with him, working through what it means to be in relation with our Sovereign.

QUICK REFERENCE CHARTS

Quick Reference Charts

Unusual Terms Found in the Psalter

Higgaion (hig-guy-**own**)	"talking/meditating," uncertain in its only application (Psalm 9), appearing before a "selah"
Maskil (mahs-**kil**)	"skilled, understanding," possibly requiring skilled playing
Miktam (mik-**tahm**)	uncertain, possibly related to "covering" or being "overwhelmed." (These few psalms concern dire circumstances.)
Mizmor (miz-**mor**)	"psalm," possibly referring to instrumental accompaniment
N^{e}ginot (neh-gee-**note**)	stringed instruments
Selah (say-**lah**)	uncertain, possibly indicating a musical break. If so, many occurrences of "selah" seem to be off by a line (in either direction).
Sh^{e}minit (sheh-mee-**neet**)	uncertain; an eight-stringed instrument or possibly tuning the instrument for male voices
Shiggaion (shig-guy-**own**)	unknown. "Wandering" (ranging tune?) and "passionate lament" are among the guesses
Shir (**sheer**)	"song," possibly referring to vocal performance
T^{e}hillah (teh-hil-**lah**)	"praise"
T^{e}phillah (teh-fil-**lah**)	"prayer"

Hebrew References to God

God: *'El* (**ale**)	"God." This is the basic word for God in its singular form. It appears one-fifth as frequently as *Elohim*. Outside the Psalter it occurs in several compound names, such as *El-Shaddai* and *El-Elyon*.
God: *'Elohim* (eh-low-**heem**)	"God," the person who defines what it is to be deity. The form with *-im* is also a plural form in Hebrew. But names are not pluralized so this is a title using the *-im* form to say that the abstract concept of deity is applied to or realized in this person. (Human kings are also referred to as "my lord" using the "plural" form. The *-im* form of *'Elohim* has nothing to do with the Trinity.)

Lord: *'Adonai* (ah-doe-**nigh**)	"My lord." This is often used as a title for God. (Its "plural" form in Hebrew is part of its being used as a title. Human kings are sometimes referred to as "my lord" using the "plural" form.)
LORD: *Yahweh* (**Yah**-way)	This is the Lord's name, meaning something like "he is/will be" (cp. Exod. 3:14). A failure to understand Jewish scribal practices led to the mistaken rendering "Jehovah," which is still widely used today. It is a convention in many translations to represent God's name with "LORD," using small caps, or sometimes with "GOD."

Types of Psalms

See above for a discussion of the types of psalms. Several psalms appear in more than one list. These are indicated by the following symbols:

(R) = Royal (R?) = Possibly Royal (I) = Instruction (L) = Liturgical

★ = appears in another unspecified list

Hymn: of Praise	8, 19 (I), 29, 33, 40★ (R), 67, 100, 103, 106★ (I), 107 (I), 113, 115 (I), 117, 134 (L), 139★ (R?), 145, 146 (I), 147, 148, 149, 150
Hymn: of Praise/ Thanksgiving	9★ (R), 34 (I), 65, 68, 104, 105, 111, 114, 118 (L), 135
Hymn: of Thanksgiving	18 (R), 30, 32 (I), 66, 92, 116, 124, 136, 138
Hymn: of the Lord's Kingship	47, 93, 95 (I), 96, 97, 98, 99★
Hymn: Zion Song	46, 48, 50 (I), 76, 84, 87, 99★, 122, 132 (R), 133 (I)
Confidence	4 (I), 11 (R?), 16, 23, 27★ (R)(L), 52 (I), 62 (I) (R?), 91 (I) (R?), 121 (R?), 125, 129★
Individual Lament	3 (R), 5, 6, 7, 9★ (R), 13, 17, 22 (R), 25★ (L), 26★ (L), 27★ (R)(L), 28★ (R) (L), 31 (R?), 35, 36, 38, 39, 40★ (R), 41 (I), 42-43, 51 (R), 54, 55, 56, 57, 59, 63 (R)(L), 64, 69, 70 (R), 71 (R), 86, 88, 102 (R?), 109, 120, 130† (I), 139★ (R?), 140, 141, 142, 143
Communal Lament‡	10, 12, 14 (I), 44, 53 (I), 58 (I), 60, 74, 77 (I), 79, 80, 83, 85, 90, 94 (R), 106★ (I), 108, 123, 126, 129★, 137
Royal	2, 3★, 9★, 18★, 20, 21, 22★, 27★ (L), 28★, 40, 45, 51★, 61, 63★, 70★, 72, 89, 94★, 101, 110, 132★, 144
Possibly Royal	1★, 31★, 62★ (I), 71★, 75 (I), 91★ (I), 102★, 121★, 139★
Liturgy	15 (I), 24 (I), 25★, 26★, 27★ (R), 28★, 118★, 131 (I), 134★
Instruction	4★, 14★, 15 (L), 19★, 24 (L), 32★, 34★, 41★, 50★, 52★, 53★, 58★, 62★ (R?), 63★ (R), 75 (R?), 77★, 78, 81, 82, 91★ (R?), 95★, 106★, 107★, 115★, 130★, 131 (L), 133★, 146★
Wisdom	1 (R?), 37, 49, 73, 112, 119, 127, 128

†The individual lamenting in Psalm 130 addresses the community at the end of the psalm.

‡Psalms 14, 53, and 77 have an individual speaking, but the issues concern the community, which may also have a speaking role in the psalm.

Common Elements of the Psalms

Explanation of Titles

Call to Praise	An invitation or command to give praise to God
Motivation to Praise	Reasons why God is praiseworthy or why people should join in praise
Praise	Worship or thanks to God for his character or deeds
Lament	A description of personal distress
Accusation	Charges made against opponents or enemies
Complaint	An expression to God of dissatisfaction with God
Claim of innocence	An assertion of not being at fault in the matter at hand
Claim of loyalty	An affirmation of commitment and desire to honor God
Confession of sin	An admission of guilt or general sinfulness, usually connected to an appeal for mercy
Petition	A request for God to act
Imprecation	A type of petition asking God to enact judicial penalties against unrighteous opponents
Motivation to listen	Reasons why God should answer the prayer
Statement of confidence	An expression of confident hope in God
Vow to praise	A promise to praise God for answering the prayer, which may include making offerings
Instruction/Wisdom	Teaching, commands, or proverbial sayings directed to the human participants or audience
Prophetic Oracles	God's word to the people or prophetic instruction
Testimony/History	An account of what God has done in a person's life or in the nation that is directed to other people

Index of Verses

An asterisk indicates that one or more verses from a series appear in another list.

Initial Appeal	4:1; 5:1-2; 6:1-3; 16:1*; 17:1-2; 28:1-2; 41:4; 54:1-2; 55:1-3; 56:1a; 57:1a; 61:1, 2; 63:1, 6; 64:1a; 69:1a, 16-18; 80:1; 83:1; 86:1a; 88:1-2; 102:1-2; 130:1-2; 140:6*; 141:1-2; 142:1-3a; 143:1-2; 146:1
Lament	6:6-7; 13:1-2; 22:6-8, 14-15; 31:9-13*; 38:5-8, 9-12, 13-14; 42:1-3, 6-7; 55:4-8; 57:4; 69:1b-3, 7-12, 19-21*; 79:4; 81:13-16*; 88:3-5, 8c-9a, 15, 17; 102:3-11; 109:22-25; 116:3-4*, 10*; 120:5; 123:5-7*; 137:1-3, 4-6; 142:4; 143:4

Accusations	3:1-2; 4:6a; 5:9; 10:3-6, 7-11; 11:1b-3; 12:1b-2; 14:1; 17:10-12; 22:12-13, 16-18; 26:10; 31:9-13★; 35:7★, 11-16★, 20-21; 36:1-4★; 38:19-20; 41:5-9; 42:10; 52:1-4★; 53:1★, 3★, 4★; 54:3; 55:10-11, 12-14, 20-21; 56:1b-2★, 5-6; 57:6; 58:1-2, 3-5; 59:3-4a, 6-7, 14-15; 62:3-4; 64:3-4★, 5-6; 69:4, 9-12★; 71:10-11; 73:4-12★; 74:4-8, 10; 79:1-3; 80:8-13; 83:2-8; 86:14; 94:4-7, 20-21; 102:8; 109:2-5, 16-18; 116:11★; 120:6-7; 129:1-2a★, 3★; 140:2-3, 4c-5; 142:3b; 143:3
Complaint	10:1; 22:1-2; 35:17a; (38:2-4)★; 42:1-3, 6-7, 9; 43:2; 44:9-12, 13-16, 19, 22, 24; 60:1-3, 9-10; 69:4★, 19-21★; 74:1, 9, 11; 79:5; 80:4-6; 85:5-6; 88:6-8b, 14, 16, 18; 89:38-46, 49; 90:3-6★, 7-11; 108:10-11
Claim of Innocence/Loyalty	7:3-5; 16:2-4, 5-6, 7-8; 17:3-5; 25:1★, 15, 21b★; 26:1b-d, 3-8, 11a; 27:8; 31:6-8; 35:13-14★; 40:9-10★; 44:17-18, 20-21; 69:4-5★;
Confession	25:7★, 11★, 18★; 38:3-5★, 17-18; 40:12★; 69:5★; 73:2-3★, 13-14★; 90:8★; 106:6-7; 130:3-4
Petition	3:7a, 8b; 4:6b; 5:8, 11; 6:4-5; 7:1, 6-8, 9-10; 9:13-14, 19-20; 10:2, 12-16; 12:1a, 3-4; 13:3; 14:7a; 16:1★; 17:6-9, 13; 20:1-5, 9; 22:11, 19-21; 25:2-7, 11, 16-21, 22; 26:1a, 2, 9, 11b; 27:7-12★; 28:2-4, 9; 30:9-10★; 31:1-5, 14-18★; 33:22; 35:1-3, 17b-c; 36:10-11, 12★; 38:1, 21-22; 39:4, 8, 10, 12★-13; 40:11-13, 16, 17★; 41:10; 43:1, 3; 44:23, 26; 51:1-2, 7-9, 10-12, 14-15, 18; 53:6; 55:9; 56:8; 59:1-2, 4b-5, 11-13; 60:5, 11; 61:4, 6-7; 64:1b, 2-4★; 65:4b; 67:1, 6-7; 68:1-3★, 4, 28, 30; 69:6, 13★-15, 29, 34; 70:1, 4, 5★; 71:1b-4, 9, 12, 18; 72:1-; 74:2-3, 18-23; 79:6, 8-9; 80:2-4★, 7, 14, 15-20; 82:8; 83:9-18; 84:8-9; 85:4, 7; 86:2★, 3a, 4a, 6, 11, 16-17★; 89:47a, 50a; 90:12-17; 94:1-2; 102:18-22, 24★; 104:34; 106:4-5, 47; 108:6, 12; 109:1, 21, 26-28a; 118:25; 120:2; 123:5★; 125:4-5; 126:4-6; 132:1, 10; 139:23-24; 140:1, 4a-b, 8; 141:3-5c, 8b, 9; 142:5-7a★; 143:7-10★, 11-12; 144:5-8, 11; 149:6-9
Motivation to Answer	3:7b-8; 5:4-6; 7:2; 13:4; 22:3-5, 9-10; 35:7-10★; 38:2-4★; 39:10b-11, 12★; 40:12★, 17★; 44:24★-25; 51:16-17, 19; 56:1b-2★; 57:1b-d★; 61:3, 5; 67:2; 70:5★; 71:5-8★, 10-11, 17; 79:7, 10a; 83:2★; 86:1b, 2★, 3a★, 3b, 4b-5, 13, 15, 17b-c; 86:10-12; 89:47b-48, 50b-51; 90:14b, 15b, 16b; 94:3; 123:1★, 2-4★, 5-7★; 141:8; 142:5-7a★; 143:5-6, 7-10★, 11-12
Imprecations	5:10; 28:4★; 31:14-18★; 35:4-6, 8★, 19; 36:12★; 40:14-15; 54:5; 55:15; 56:7★; 58:6-8; 69:22-28; 70:2-3; 71:13; 79:10b-12; 104:35; 109:6-15, 19-20, 28b-29; 120:3-4; 129:5-8b; 137:7-9; 139:19-20; 140:9-11; 141:9
Vows	7:17★; 13:6; 14:7b-c; 22:22; 26:12b; 30:12b; 34:1; 35:9-10, 18; 43:4; 51:13; 54:6; 56:12; 57:9-10★; 61:8; 63:2-5; 65:1★; 66:13-15; 69:30; 71:14-16★; 73:28★; 75:9★; 79:13; 86:12; 104:33; 108:1b-3; 109:30; 111:1b-c; 116:13-14, 17-18; 144:9-10
Statements of Confidence	3:3-6, 8; 4:2-5, 7-8; 5:3-7, 12; 6:8-10; 7:11-13,★ 14-16,★ 17★; 9:15-18; 10:17-18; 11:1a&7, 4-6★; 12:7-8; 13:5; 16:9-11; 17:14-15; 20:6★, 7-8; 21:7-12; 22:25-31; 23:1-6; 25:1★; 26:12a; 27:1-6, 10, 13; 28:5, 8; 31:19-20; 33:20-21; 34:2; 36:5-9★; 38:15-16; 39:7; 41:11-13; 42:(4), 8; 44:4-8; 46:1-9, 11; 48:8; 51:3-6; 52:8-9; 54:4; 55:16-19, 23e; 56:3-4, 9, 10-11; 57:1b-d,★ 2-3, 7-8; 58:9-11; 59:8, 9, 10, 16, 17; 60:4, 12; 62:1-2, 5-6, 7; 63:7-10; 64:7-9, 10; 68:21-23, 29, 31; 69:13a, 35-36; 71:1a, 5-7★, 14-16★, 19-21, 22-24; 73:23-28★; 75:9-10; 86:7; 88:9b-c, 13; 91:2; 92:9-11, 12-15; 94:12-15★, 22-23; 102:12-17, 28★; 108:1a, 13; 115:12-18; 116:15-16; 121:1-8; 123:1★, 2-4★; 125:1-2★; 129:8c; 130:5-6; 134:3; 138:1-2a★, 6-8; 140:6★-7, 12-13; 141:5d-7; 142:7b; 144:12-14, 15

Call to Praise	2:10-12★; 9:11-12; 22:23; 29:1-2; 30:4-5; 33:1-3; 34:3; 47:1, 6; 48:12-13; 66:1-2, 5, 8, 16; 67:3-5; 68:3★, 4(-6), 32-34; 81:1-3; 92:1-3; 95:1-2, 6; 96:1-3, 7-9, 10-12; 97:1; 98:1a, 4-6, 7-9a; 99:1b, 1d, 2b-3, 5, 9; 100:1-2, 4; 103:1-2, 20-22; 104:1a, 35b; 105:1-4, 5-6; 106:1-3; 107:1-3; 111:1a; 112:1a; 113:1-3; 116:12★; 117:1; 118:1-4, 29; 132:6-9; 134:1-2; 135:1-3, 19-20; 136:1-3, 26; 138:45; 145:21; 147:1, 7, 12; 148:1-13★; 149:1-3, 5; 150:1-6
Praise	8:1-8★; 9:1-10; 18:1-50★; 19:1-6; 21:1-6, 13; 24:1-2; 28:6-7★; 30:1-3, 6-12★; 31:21-22; 33:4-11★; 34:4★, 6★; (39:5); 40:1-3, 5; 44:1-3; 46:4-6, 8-9; 47:2-4★, 5, 7-9; 48:1-3, 4-7, 9-10; 54:7★; 56:13★; 57:5, 10★, 11; 65:1-2, 5-13; 66:3-4★, 6-7★, 9-12★, 17-20★; 68:5-6★, 11-14★, 15-18★, 19-20, 24-27★, 35; 74:12-17; 75:1; 76:1-10; 77:11b-20; 84:1-3, 11; 85:1-3, 10-13; 86:8-10; 89:1-2, 5-14, 52, 53; 90:1-2, 3-6★; 92:4-7, 8; 93:1-5; 95:3-5; 96:4-6★, 13★; 97:2-6, 9★; 99:1a, 1c, 2a, 4, 6-8; 100:5★; 102:25-27★; 103:3-6, 19; 104:1b-30, 31-32; 105:7-45; 106:48; 107:4-9★, 10-16★, 17-22★, 23-32★, 33-41★; 108:4★, 5; 109:31★; 111:2-9; 113:4-9; 114:1-8★; 116:5-6★, 8-9; 118:14★, 16★, 21★, 22-24, 28; 124:1-5, 6-9; 126:1-3; 129:2b★, 4; 135:4-7, 8-14, 21; 136:4-25; 138:1-3★; 139:1-18; 144:1-2, 3-4; 145:1-20; 146:2, 5-9★, 10; 147:2-6, 8-9★, 13-20★; 148:14
Motivation to Praise	22:24; 29:3-9, 10-11; 47:2-4★; 48:14; 54:7★; 67:4b-c★; 68:5-6★; 81:4-5; 95:7a-c; 96:4-6★, 13★; 98:1b-3, 9b-d; 99:5c★, 9c★; 100:5★; 108:4; 117:2; 147:13-20★; 148:6★, 13★; 149:4
Instruction/ Wisdom	1:1-6; 2:1-12; 7:11-13,★ 14-16★; 8:1b-7★; 11:4-6★; 14:2-6; 15:1-5★; 19:7-9,10-14; 24:3-6★, 7-10★; 25:8-10★, 12-14★; 31:23-24; 32:1-2, 6-7, 8-9★, 10-11; 33:4-11★, 12-15, 16-19; 34:5, 7, 8-14, 15-18, 19-21; 36:1-4★, 5-9★; 37:1-40; 39:6★; 40:4, 6-8★; 41:1-3; 42:5, 11; 43:5; 49:1-20; 50:1-6★; 52:1-4★, 5-7; 53:1-6; 55:22-23; 62:8, 9-10; 63:11; 65:4; 66:18★; 68:15-18; 69:31-33; 73:1-28; 75:2-5, 6-8; 76:11; 77:1-11a; 78:1-72★; 81:6-16; 82:1-7; 84:4, 5-7, 10, 12; 85:8-9; 87:1-7; 89:15-18; 91:1, 3-8, 9-13; 94:8-11, 12-15★; 95:7d-11; 97:7, 10-12; 100:3; 103:7-18; 107:42-43; 109:31★; 111:10; 112:1b-10; 114:5-8★; 115:1-8, 9-11; 116:5-6★, 7; 118:8-10★; 119:1-176; 125:1-2★, 3; 127:1-2, 3-5; 128:1-3, 4-6; 130:7-8; 131:3; 133:1-3; 135:15-18; 144:15; 146:3-4, 5-9★; 147:8-9★, 10-11
Prophetic Oracles	12:5-6; 20:6★; 25:8-10★, 12-14★; 27:14; 32:8-9★; 39:6★; 46:10; 50:7-23; 60:6-8; 89:3-4, 19-37; 91:14-16; 108:7-9; 110:1-7; 121:3-8; 132:2-5, 11-12, 13-16, 17-18
Testimony/History	30:6-12★; 32:3-5; 34:4★, 6★; 39:1-3, 9; 40:7-10★; 65:3★; 66:6-7★, 9-12★, 17-20★; 68:7-10, 11-14, 24-27★; 73:2-28★; 78:9-72★; 94:16-19; 97:8-9★; 101:1-8★; 102:23-28★; 105:12-41★; 106:6-46; 107:4-9★, 10-16★, 17-22★, 23-32★, 33-41★; 114:1-4★; 116:1-9★, 10-11★; 118:5-7, 8-21★; 120:1; 124:1-5, 6-9; 129:1-4★

THE PSALMS

Psalm 1

THEME: A righteous individual is established and prospers by attending to God's Word.

TYPE: Wisdom, possibly royal.

AUTHOR: Unknown.

BACKGROUND: Most Israelites did not own scrolls and did not have a copy of the law of Moses (Genesis through Deuteronomy). Only priests, scribes, perhaps the very rich, and the king had regular access to the written Word of God. Deuteronomy 17:18–20 instructed the king to make his own copy of the Law. He was to read it every day to learn to fear and obey God so that he and his descendants would prosper. Psalm 1 admonishes him to read God's Law regularly to differentiate between wickedness and righteousness in order to prosper, and it implies the Psalter should be read in a similar light.

STRUCTURE: The psalm has three parts, each containing a contrast. Verses 1–2 contrast the influence one chooses, the counsel of the wicked or the Law of God. Verses 3–4 contrast a well-watered tree with chaff as an image of the enduring strength that comes from the choice in verses 1–2. Verses 5–6 directly contrast the fate of the wicked and the righteous.

SPECIAL NOTES: *Chaff* refers to the dry fragments of the shell-type coverings of grain seeds. After the coverings are broken off, the light chaff and the heavy seeds are separated by tossing them into the air so that the wind blows away the chaff.

Law. The Psalms' poetry typically uses different words with similar meanings to refer to the same idea. Here the word *Law*, or *Torah*, is used in both parts of verse 2. Torah is also the Hebrew title for the "Law of Moses."

Joseph Sohm–Visions of America/Getty Images

REFLECTION: Like the theme song of an album, Psalm 1 sets a tone for reading the Psalter; it places us at a fork in life's road. We're invited by way of metaphors to consider the paths and where they lead. One is living, flourishing—a vibrant fruit tree; the other is dead—empty hulls, chaff blowing away in the wind. Like poetic commentary on Deuteronomy 30:19–20, "I have set before you life and death, blessings and curses. Now choose life.... For the LORD is your life," righteousness and wickedness parallel life and death. Everyone with access to the written Word of God should follow the example in the psalm. Study and meditation are necessary for knowing God's ways, but in turn God "watches over the way of the righteous." God says through this song, "Stay in the way of the righteous. I will plant you like a well-watered tree, and you will be blessed."

Psalm 2

PlanetArt

THEME: The Lord has established his king on Zion. Worship the Lord; honor the king.

TYPE: Royal.

AUTHOR: Unknown.

BACKGROUND: Likely used when crowning the king, perhaps first for Solomon and subsequently for all the sons of David. But it was not necessarily limited to the king's coronation ceremony.

STRUCTURE: The psalm has four main sections with three verses each. Stanza 1 (vv. 1–3) poses the problem of planned rebellion. Stanza 2 (vv. 4–6) responds with the Lord's self-assured attitude. Stanza 3 (vv. 7–9) extends that perspective with the king's confidence in the Lord's support. Finally, stanza 4 (vv. 10–12) admonishes the people of the proper response to the Lord and the king.

SPECIAL NOTES: The psalm makes several points by reporting the words of different people. Foreign rulers speak in section 1; the Lord speaks in section 2; the king speaks and quotes the Lord in section 3. Section 4 is like the words of a herald addressing the people.

REFLECTION: We may reflect on the psalm with a question for each stanza. Stanza 1: What do people think they can do? Stanza 2: What does God think of their ideas? Stanza 3: Who is in charge? Stanza 4: So how should we respond?

When plans are being laid and people are taking sides but the outcome is not known, it may be tempting to follow a particular group. But the greatest freedom and security are found under the authority of God.

Psalm 3

THEME: The king is very confident in God's protection, despite many opponents who say God will not deliver him.

TYPE: Individual lament, royal.

AUTHOR: A psalm (*mizmor*) of David. When he fled from his son Absalom.

BACKGROUND: Second Samuel 15–18 records when David fled from his rebelling son Absalom to the wilderness of Judah. Absalom succeeded in taking the throne temporarily but was later killed in battle.

STRUCTURE: The psalm has five sections. It begins with a complaint, verses 1–2, then moves to its main element in two statements of confidence in verses 3–4 and 5–6. Verse 7 delivers the petition. In conclusion the king affirms God and prays for his blessing on the people in verse 8.

SPECIAL NOTES: David had to leave Jerusalem, but God heard him from his "holy mountain," a reference to Jerusalem that also echoes Psalm 2:6. While the picture surely looked bleak for David when he had to flee the capital city, he expressed a great degree of confidence in his ability to lie down and sleep in verse 5, a picture that occurs only here and in Psalm 4:8. It has led some to view Psalm 3 as a morning prayer and Psalm 4 as an evening prayer.

AP/Wide World Photos

REFLECTION: Immediately after the first two introductory psalms, a coup d'état in the royal family catches us by surprise. Rebellion and conflict come not from the nations in Psalm 2 nor from a rival king, but from betrayal within David's own house. The anointed king, far from ruling with a rod of iron or dashing enemies like pottery, flees to old familiar haunts in the wilderness. There he remembers the Lord's deliverance from the hand of Saul. He remembers the Lord, his shield, and turns to him.

How often has the greatest grief come from within our own families, our own communities of faith—allies turning antagonists, friends becoming betrayers? David has preceded us in such circumstances and given us words.

Psalm 4

© U.P.images/www.istockphoto.com

THEME: God hears the godly; David will entrust himself to God.

TYPE: Mixed: confidence, instruction. The initial call for deliverance and presence of opponents in the psalm suggests it is a lament, but the bulk of the psalm expresses confidence in God. Half the psalm does not address God but acts as instruction to the people.

AUTHOR: A psalm (*mizmor*) of David. For the director of music. With stringed instruments.

BACKGROUND: The specific background is uncertain, but the phrase "lie down and sleep" provides a link to Psalm 3, which is traditionally related to David's conflict with Absalom (2 Sam. 15–18).

STRUCTURE: The psalm has five sections. The psalm begins with an initial appeal for God to listen in verse 1. Then it shifts to address the people with a rhetorical question in verse 2 and answers the question by proclaiming confidence that God hears the "faithful servant" (perhaps originally meaning the king) in verse 3. In the third section, the psalmist admonishes the people to fidelity to the Lord (vv. 4–5). Next he contrasts the hopeless thoughts of others with a confident request for the Lord's attention (vv. 6–7). In the last section, the psalmist makes himself an example of trusting the Lord (v. 8).

SPECIAL NOTES: Lying down to sleep as a picture of confidence occurs only here and in Psalm 3:5. It has led some to view Psalm 3 as a morning prayer and Psalm 4 as an evening prayer.

Paul quotes the Greek translation of Psalm 4:4 in Ephesians 4:26.

REFLECTION: One of the early church fathers, Chrysostom, once said that if he could preach to the whole world, he would choose Psalm 4:2.† This verse presents God's perennial lament: "How long will you men turn my glory into shame? How long will you love delusions and seek false gods?" How profound that the God of the universe should lament to us.

Also, the psalmist, while in the nexus between distress and deliverance, chooses to stand in confidence: he "hears when I call to him" (v. 3); "You alone, LORD, make me dwell in safety" (v. 8). His fear, mentioned in the previous psalm, has subsided. With confidence he prays, "Give me relief from my distress" (v. 1), and lies down to rest in safety. Confidence joined to faith is a great sleep aid.

†See Thomas Brooks (1608–80), *The Complete Works of Thomas Brooks*, vol. 4, ed. Alexander Balloch Grosart (Edinburgh: J. Nichol, 1867), 35.

Psalm 5

THEME: God does not tolerate the wicked but protects those who trust him.

TYPE: Individual lament.

AUTHOR: A psalm (*mizmor*) of David. For the director of music. For pipes.

BACKGROUND: No specifics are known, but the psalm indicates that David has adversaries who speak lies and plot harm against him.

STRUCTURE: The initial appeal in verses 1–2 is completed by the last verse of the psalm. In between are two stanzas of seven lines each (vv. 3–7 and vv. 8–11; vv. 3, 7, 10, and 11 each contain two poetic lines). The first seven-line stanza asserts the basis for the psalmist's petition; the second makes the petition.

SPECIAL NOTES: Mention of the temple in verse 7 may imply that the title of the psalm be understood as being for the Davidic heir rather than for David himself, since the temple was not built in David's lifetime. David, however, might be referring to the Lord's heavenly temple.

Paul quotes the Greek translation of Psalm 5:9 in Romans 3:13a (as well as referring to Pss. 14:1–3 and 140:3 in the same part of Rom. 3).

REFLECTION: A holy God will not put up with the wicked. But the psalmist can approach God with reverence because of his great love. While it is preferable for the wicked to repent, God is asked to show his justice by giving the wicked their dues. Dealing out consequences for evil instructs all of society in justice. The unrepentant do not get a pass. Taking refuge in God entails more than wanting benefits from him; it implies allegiance to and dependence on him.

Psalm 6

THEME: The psalmist, in grave physical distress, prays for healing and expresses confidence that enemies will be refuted.

TYPE: Individual lament.

AUTHOR: A psalm (*mizmor*) of David. For the director of music. With stringed instruments. According to *sheminith*.

BACKGROUND: The psalmist appears to be sick, concerned about dying, and harassed by enemies.

STRUCTURE: The angst of the psalm condenses in a centered line (v. 6a): "I am worn out from my groaning." The two stanzas on either side of the center line mirror each other in length. Stanza 1 (three line pairs in vv. 1–3) is the initial appeal with a description of the psalmist's troubles. Stanza 2 (two line pairs in vv. 4–5) petitions God for rescue from death. Stanza 3 (two line pairs in vv. 6b–7) laments the distress of the psalmist. Finally, stanza 4 (three line pairs in vv. 8–10) expresses confidence in God.

SPECIAL NOTES: *Sheminith* may refer to an eight-stringed instrument or a musical style.

Although the psalm moves to an expression of confidence in eight verses, the center line expresses the psalmist's weariness from waiting so long, which indicates that he found no quick solution.

Jesus alludes to Psalm 6:8 in Matthew 7:23.

© Diane Diederich/www.istockphoto.com

REFLECTION: In this psalm weeping is synonymous with a cry for mercy: "The LORD has heard my weeping" (v. 8).

Images of extreme distress take the psalmist to the edges of confidence and far from restful comfort: "I am faint ... my bones are in agony.... My soul is in deep anguish.... I am worn out from my groaning.... I flood my bed with weeping.... My eyes grow weak with sorrow." He cries out, "How long, LORD, how long?"—one of humanity's two primordial laments, "How long?" and "Why?" These laments are questions that continue to resound in the hearts of God's people struggling like the psalmist to live out their faith in the midst of pain and suffering. Here God provides language for us to voice our physical and spiritual anguish, to cry out for relief—all in the context of faith.

When we find ourselves in similar states, we can rest in the awareness that the psalmist and our Lord himself have preceded us there and left us words to help locate ourselves, to hang on to faith, and to grab hold of God.

Psalm 7

THEME: God is a righteous judge who delivers the innocent.

TYPE: Individual lament.

AUTHOR: A *shiggaion* of David, which he sang to the Lord concerning Cush, a Benjamite.

BACKGROUND: Unclear. Cush the Benjamite is not mentioned elsewhere in the Bible. But the context of the psalm makes it appear that the psalmist is both falsely accused and on the run from attack.

STRUCTURE: Rather than the general request to listen that begins many laments, this psalm goes straight to the heart of the problem, petitioning God for rescue from being torn to pieces in verses 1–2. Verses 3–5 protest innocence, inviting the enemy to win if the psalmist is guilty. Verses 6–8 and 9–10 petition God to act in just wrath. Verses 11–13 and 14–16 both express the psalmist's confidence and offer instruction about God punishing the wicked. Their wicked plans and deeds come back on their own heads. Finally, the psalmist vows to praise the Lord in verse 17.

© Johan Swanepoel/www.istockphoto.com

SPECIAL NOTES: So sure is the psalmist of his innocence that he calls a curse on himself if he is in the wrong. The central stanza of the poem is the appeal for vindication in verses 8b–9.

The meaning of *shiggaion* in the title is unclear, though it may refer to the idea of lament.

REFLECTION: Verse 9 expresses the heart of imprecation—a prayer for judgment, for punishment. David holds everyone, including himself, to the fiercest standard of impartial justice and clearly considers himself subject to the righteous judge who "probes minds and hearts" (v. 9) and "displays his wrath every day" (v. 11). From this place and not from spite or personal vendetta, David the warrior king, a type of Christ, prays for judgment of evil.

Martin Luther wrote that whoever prays, "Hallowed be thy name, thy kingdom come, thy will be done," must also pray against all those in opposition to this and say: "Curses, maledictions and disgrace upon every other name and every other kingdom. May they be ruined and torn apart and may all their schemes and wisdom and plans run aground."† If we would ask of the Lord, "Teach us to pray," and if we would transcend in our prayers above mere sentiments of spite and personal vendettas, we must consider how to stand in this same way for the kingdom of righteousness in the world and for good to finally and truly triumph over all evil.

†Martin Luther, *Luther's Works*, ed. Jaroslav Pelikan (St. Louis: Concordia, 1956), 21:101.

Psalm 8

PhotoDisc

THEME: The Lord reigns in the heavens; he has set humanity to rule the earth.

TYPE: Hymn of praise.

AUTHOR: A psalm (*mizmor*) of David. For the director of music. According to *gittith*.

BACKGROUND: The psalmist meditates on the majesty of the heavens and is awed by God's concern and the special place he has given mere humans.

STRUCTURE: The same refrain opens and closes the psalm, proclaiming the majesty of the Lord's name. The remaining lines divide into two stanzas of four lines each. The first of these (vv. 1d–4) proclaims the Lord's glory as seen in the heavens and in contrast to mere humans. The second (vv. 5–8) declares humanity's dominion over the earth.

SPECIAL NOTES: Psalm 8:4–6 is cited in Hebrews 2:6–8, arguing that it was necessary for Jesus to be made "a little lower than the angels" as part of "put[ting] everything under his feet" (v. 8 NIV). The phrase "son of man" (NIV) can simply mean "human beings" (TNIV) but is also used at times as a title. If it were a title here, it could represent the king's special reflections and be all the more appropriate, though not necessary, as an application to Jesus.

Jesus quotes Psalm 8:2 in Matthew 21:16; Paul quotes Psalm 8:6 in 1 Corinthians 15:27.

It is not known whether *gittith* in the title is a musical instrument or a musical style.

REFLECTION: The moon is about 2,160 miles (3,476 km) across and 238,857 miles (384,403 km) away from the earth. We are 93 million miles from the sun, into which 1,300,000 earths would fit. We are about 24 trillion miles from the next nearest star. The North Star is 90 times that distance away. There are billions of stars in our galaxy. The scale of the solar system and the galaxy staggers the mind. The psalmist did not know the distances but understood the comparison "like the sand of the sea" as equally mind-boggling. With or without knowing the numbers, the brilliant display of stars in the clear night sky (especially unhindered by pollution and city lights) is amazing. How easily it makes one feel small! Yet, as small and insignificant as we may seem against such a cosmic backdrop, we are rulers—rulers of this planet, a little lower than the angels. Yet rulers under a majestic Lord. May we rule wisely!

Psalm 9

THEME: God has defeated our enemies in the past, so we can implore him to deliver us again and trust that he will do justice.

TYPE: Royal: praise/thanksgiving and lament.

AUTHOR: A psalm (*mizmor*) of David. For the director of music. To the tune of "The Death of the Son."

BACKGROUND: Although the speaker is singular, using "I" and "me," he is clearly concerned with national issues, since the psalm refers to the "nations" (9:5, 15 and 10:16). It is most reasonable to see the king as the main speaker with the community present as well. Other communal laments also begin with a praise section before stating the distress of the moment.

STRUCTURE: The psalm has two major sections. Section 1 (9:1–12) centers on praise. The psalmist praises the Lord in verses 1–2 and calls on the people to praise him in verses 11–12. Between these are two stanzas of four verses each. The first (vv. 3–6) recalls God's defeat of the enemies. The second (vv. 7–10) praises God for his just rule of all the earth.

Section 2 begins (vv. 13–14) and ends (vv. 19–20) with petitions for God to act and deliver from the enemies who are a current threat. The verses in between (vv. 15–18) are a statement of confidence that God will enact justice and attend to the afflicted.

SPECIAL NOTES: Psalms 9 and 10 together form a partial alphabetic acrostic. An alphabetic acrostic is a poem that begins lines at regular intervals with successive letters of the alphabet. A few letters of the alphabet are missing from the pattern, and a couple occur in reverse order. Still Psalm 9 uses the beginning of the alphabet and Psalm 10 picks up where Psalm 9 leaves off, with *L* or *lamed*, and continues on to complete the alphabet. This encourages us to read the two psalms together, where we actually find three major sections—9:1–12; 9:13–20; and Psalm 10.

REFLECTION: See Psalm 10.

Psalm 10

THEME: Though the wicked afflict the weak, the psalmist remains confident that the Lord pays attention, and he can trust in God's rule.

TYPE: Communal lament.

AUTHOR: Probably a psalm (*mizmor*) of David continued from Psalm 9. Psalm 10 has no title of its own, though most psalms in book 1 do.

BACKGROUND: The societal problems of the wicked oppressing the weak and defenseless stand in the background of this psalm. The reference to the nations in verse 16 may imply that these evildoers are foreigners in Israel.

STRUCTURE: Verses 1–2 question the Lord for being uninvolved when the wicked hunt down the weak. Verses 17–18 conclude with a statement of confidence that the Lord hears the afflicted and defends the oppressed. Between these are three stanzas of six lines each. The first two of these (vv. 3–6 and 7–11) describe the scheming of the wicked and end with their confident thoughts of prosperity without adversity (v. 6) and the belief that God doesn't pay any attention (v. 11). The third six-line stanza (vv. 12–16) petitions the Lord to rise up and judge the wicked and affirms that he does see the afflicted and rules all.

SPECIAL NOTES: See the notes in Psalm 9 on the literary unity of Psalms 9 and 10.

Romans 3:14 quotes the Greek translation of Psalm 10:7.

REFLECTION: Reminiscent of Psalm 2, we find the wicked scheming and are given a window into their thoughts. They think God is out of the picture—there is no God, or if there is, he pays no attention. They use deceit to take advantage of people and believe they will face no consequences and always have it easy. In Psalm 73 even Asaph struggles with thinking the wicked may be right.

But Psalm 9 provides the proper backdrop and an established approach to prayer in the Psalms. Psalm 9 praises God for his good character in precisely the area of complaint. The psalmist affirms what God is truly like as part of the dissonance of the current experience of the wicked. Circumstances do not define God's character. They move us to call on his character. They call for appropriate consequences for the wicked (cf. 10:2) and protection for the unfortunate.

Psalm 11

Copyright 1995–2010 Phoenix Data Systems

THEME: We can take refuge in the Lord because he rules righteously from heaven, judging the wicked and favoring the upright.

TYPE: Confidence, possibly royal

AUTHOR: Of David. For the director of music.

BACKGROUND: The psalmist apparently faces some danger, and possibly the king has one or more advisers counseling him to flee.

STRUCTURE: The thought of trust in the Lord that begins in verse 1a is completed in the last verse. Two sections stand in between. Verses 1b–3 use a rhetorical question to report the discouraging thoughts of an adviser who says to flee. Verses 4–6 answer this question by asserting that God rules in heaven, scrutinizes humanity, and judges the wicked.

REFLECTION: Fleeing from danger, as David did from Saul and later from Absalom, is unadvisable in these circumstances. The only safety for the psalmist is in committing his way to the Lord.

"Look," "observe," and "examine" are key verbs in this psalm. The psalmist invites us to look into the shadows and see the wicked bending their bows to shoot the righteous, and to look and see the very foundations of the mountains crumbling, offering no safety even if he did fly away to them. Alas, what can the righteous do? Where is his refuge? The central verse, the pivotal picture, invites us to look up, to see the Lord on his throne. He is one who sees all and rains down fiery coals and burning sulfur on the wicked—those hiding in the shadows. In the final picture "the upright will see his face." This very thought seemed to be echoed by Christ on the Mount of Olives as he spoke a blessing on the pure in heart, ". . . they will see God" (Matt. 5:8). The apostle John reminds us that it is this hope that also keeps us pure (1 John 3:2–3).

Psalm 12

THEME: The psalmist prays for the Lord's protection of the needy from deceivers.

TYPE: Communal lament.

AUTHOR: A psalm (*mizmor*) of David. For the director of music. According to *sheminith*.

BACKGROUND: Social injustice and widespread deceit stand in the background as concerns of the psalmist.

STRUCTURE: The psalm divides into four stanzas of two verses each. Verses 1–2 briefly petition the Lord for help and mainly make accusations about a deceitful society. Verses 3–4 petition the Lord to destroy those who speak falsely. Verses 5–6 contain a promise from the Lord to act and an affirmation by the psalmist. Lastly, verses 7–8 express confidence in the Lord's protection despite the surrounding wickedness.

SPECIAL NOTES: Verses 5–6 are like a prophetic word delivered in the midst of the psalm, where the prophet delivers God's message and then praises the reliability of the Lord's word.

Sheminith may refer to an eight-stringed instrument or a musical style.

© Olly/www.istockphoto.com

REFLECTION: In the center of this psalm, the false words of the boastful and the pure, reliable words of the Lord clash. Both the needy psalmist's cry for help and the words of the proud rouse the Lord, "'Because the poor are plundered and the needy groan, I will now arise,' says the LORD. 'I will protect them from those who malign them'" (v. 5). In the Lord's words the psalmist finds safety and protection, though depravity is honored among the wicked and the proud freely strut about. By his voice, his words, the battle is won.

Psalm **13**

THEME: The psalmist persists in trusting the Lord despite a long delay in being answered.

TYPE: Individual lament.

AUTHOR: A psalm (*mizmor*) of David. For the director of music.

BACKGROUND: The psalmist has been in difficulty for a long period of time and fears that he may die.

STRUCTURE: The psalm has three stanzas of two verses each. Verses 1–2 are lament. Verses 3–4 are petition and motivation to answer. Verses 5–6 are a statement of confidence and vow to praise the Lord.

SPECIAL NOTES: The phrase "hide your face" is a picture of someone refusing to listen, someone holding court who will not grant an audience to a petitioner. The psalmist feels that the Lord will not show him his face, meaning that he has not been listening to his prayers.

REFLECTION: What a beautiful example is set for us in this lament! Assurance of faith comes by struggling to hold on to God by faith even in the darkest of circumstances. By his very complaint that God has forgotten him, the psalmist gives evidence that his faith has turned him to God and not away. So juxtaposed, the seen (evidence recounted) and the unseen (evidence longed for) collide together in the psalmist's struggle to see the promise; his face pressed hard to heaven, he strains to see what has been hidden. From us, too, God may redemptively hide his face, and we may then follow the psalmist's example.

Psalm 14

THEME: The Lord really does see the wicked even if they do not believe in him; so continue to trust in the Lord.

TYPE: Mixed: instruction, lament.

AUTHOR: Of David. For the director of music.

BACKGROUND: The psalm offers insight on the problem of wicked people who have success for a time.

Concerning its type, the psalm acts like a court scene. The fool is indicted and sentenced. Here, similar to prophetic instruction, the psalmist offers the Lord's perspective as he observes evildoers. But it also has elements similar to a lament. The indictments are like the accusations of a lament. It has a statement of confidence. And like many laments, it ends with a petition for God to save.

STRUCTURE: Stanza 1 (v. 1) describes the fool. Stanza 2 (vv. 2–3) describes the Lord evaluating humans. The center line (v. 4a) expresses incredulity by asking rhetorically how wicked fools can be so ignorant. The next stanza (vv. 4b–6) indicts these evildoers and pronounces judgment on them. The last stanza (v. 7) calls for the Lord to enact his judgment and deliver Israel.

SPECIAL NOTES: Most people in the ancient world believed in many gods. Here the wicked are dangerous because they have a practical atheism, believing no one will call them to account.

Paul quotes Psalm 14:1–3 in Romans 3:10–12.

Psalms 14 and 53 are nearly identical.

REFLECTION: Perspective can make a big difference. A change of camera angle might change opinion about a sports play. A new point of view may sway a debate. Though some people may seem intimidating in their confidence, new information can seemingly change everything. In this psalm we see the confident perspective of the "fool." Then God's perspective "changes everything."

Psalm 15

THEME: Those who may approach the Lord are those who live in integrity.

TYPE: Liturgy, instruction.

AUTHOR: A psalm (*mizmor*) of David.

BACKGROUND: Psalm 15 may have been recited as worshipers approached Jerusalem. The priests or gatekeepers would call out the opening question, and those approaching the city would respond with the answer. Then the priests or gatekeepers would respond with the final line.

STRUCTURE: The first part poses the question that the rest of the psalm answers. It asks who is worthy to approach the Lord in his holy dwelling. The character of such a person is described in six more two-part lines in verses 2–5b. The last two-part line pronounces a blessing on those with such good character (v. 5c–d).

SPECIAL NOTES: The question-and-answer motif serves to instruct the members of the community. The technique appears elsewhere (Ex. 13:14; Deut. 6:20; Ps. 24) and also became a regular part of the Passover celebration.

A blameless walk (v. 2) is also referred to in Psalms 26:1, 11; 84:11; 101:2, 6; and 119:1.

REFLECTION: Since the psalm ends with a promise for the one who does "these things," it is compelling to reflect on how well we do them. As a liturgy about being able to enter God's presence, such self-reflection is well suited for communion services. In this setting our reflection may lead to confession. We also realize that our affirmation to enter his presence depends on our participation in his righteousness.

Psalm 16

© Lukasz Kulicki/www.istockphoto.com

THEME: The psalmist proclaims loyalty to the Lord and confidence in his protection.

TYPE: Confidence.

AUTHOR: A *miktam* of David.

BACKGROUND: Israel did not completely remove the influence of those who worshiped other gods when they entered the land under Joshua. The temptation to trust other gods persisted throughout the kingdoms of Israel and Judah. Here the psalmist rejects those influences.

STRUCTURE: A single line of petition (v. 1) is followed by four stanzas in a line pattern of 3-2-2-3 (vv. 2–4, 5–6, 7–8, and 9–11). The last line of each of the three-line stanzas is a three-part line (tricolon).

Verse 1 asks God for safety, a petition that is bound up with the psalmist's reliance on God alone. Verses 2–4 contain an affirmation of loyalty to the Lord and refusal to worship other gods. Verses 5–6 address the Lord as the psalmist's true, spiritual inheritance and credit him with good gifts in life. Verses 7–8 praise the Lord for his guidance and affirm that the psalmist looks steadfastly to him. Finally, verses 9–11 express the psalmist's joy and the confidence that the Lord will protect him from death.

SPECIAL NOTES: Read as a royal psalm, this psalm has the king stating his confidence in God's protection, perhaps in battle, and ability to preserve his life. Peter and Paul (Acts 2:25–28; 13:35) extend this royal interpretation to Jesus, the ultimate Davidic heir in whom the psalm is fulfilled, not in preserving Jesus from death, but in his conquering death through the resurrection.

The reflection that the Lord is David's inheritance (v. 5) stands out all the more if we assume that the king is speaking, for he was very wealthy. Otherwise the portion of each tribe was its allotment of land, while the Levites received support from the other tribes as their portion (Num. 18:6–14; Deut. 18:1; Josh. 18:7; cf. Pss. 73:26; 119:57; 142:5).

REFLECTION: The psalmist has taken refuge in God alone, and that has made all the difference. "Keep me safe" is the psalmist's petition. What follows is the psalmist envisioning that safety and the resultant trust—a delightful picture of God watching over the way of the righteous, the one whose eyes are always watching God.

Psalm 17

THEME: On the basis of innocence, the psalmist appeals to God for protection from dangerous enemies and finds satisfaction in God.

SPECIAL NOTES: The "apple of your eye" (v. 8) is an English expression; it refers to the pupil, which one naturally tries to protect.

TYPE: Individual lament.

AUTHOR: A prayer of David.

BACKGROUND: The psalmist is in danger from enemies who have hunted him down.

STRUCTURE: The psalm has five stanzas of three or four lines each. Verses 1–2 are the initial appeal for God to listen. Verses 3–5 are the psalmist's claim of innocence. In verses 6–9 the psalmist petitions for protection from enemies. Verses 10–12 contain an accusation against the enemies. The last stanza begins with another petition in verse 13, then proceeds to a statement of confidence in verses 14–15.

REFLECTION: "My mouth has not transgressed" and "my feet have not stumbled" are bold declarations of innocence. The wicked, like crouching lions hungry for prey, seek to destroy the psalmist not because of his sin but because he is righteous; thus he protests because of his innocence, "Keep me as the apple of your eye" (v. 8). His petition is for protection and deliverance, but his deeper longing is for his satisfaction—"I will . . . see your face; . . . I will be satisfied with seeing your likeness" (v. 15).

Can we make such bold protests on our own behalf? What is preventing us? Where does our satisfaction ultimately come from?

Psalm 18

© Peter Anderson/www.istockphoto.com

THEME: David praises God for deliverance from his enemies.

TYPE: Royal, hymn of thanksgiving.

AUTHOR: Of David the servant of the Lord. For the director of music. He sang to the Lord the words of this song when the Lord delivered him from the hand of all his enemies and the hand of Saul.

BACKGROUND: The historical setting for Psalm 18 is recorded in 2 Samuel 21. This chapter records a punishment on the house of Saul as well as several battles with the Philistines in which the sons of the giant Goliath were killed. Second Samuel 22 then quotes this psalm in very similar, though not quite identical, form.

STRUCTURE: In the stanzas in the first twenty-one lines (vv. 1–19), David affirms his trust in the Lord and describes how God acted from heaven in response to his prayers. The next ten lines (vv. 20–29) proclaim the mutual loyalty of the Lord and David. David kept God's ways, and as the Lord is loyal to those who are loyal, he helped David. The last twenty-one lines (vv. 30–50) describe how the Lord empowered him and he overcame his enemies then ends with a stanza of praise.

SPECIAL NOTES: Though the psalm is about David in particular, its continuing relevance is evident in the final verse, which extends God's loyal love to his anointed, to the descendants of David. Just as all Israelites could place themselves in the tradition of those God had delivered from Egypt, so David's heirs, at least those faithful to the Lord, could place themselves in the tradition of God's deliverance of David. As the head of the kingdom, the Davidic heirs would be protected by God, and that protection would benefit the whole community.

The horn imagery comes from bulls (not the ram's horn used as a trumpet), possibly from two bulls fighting each other with their horns. So the horn of the wicked or of the righteous symbolizes their strength or victory. Compare Psalms 22:21; 75:4–5, 10; 89:17; 92:10; 112:9; 148:14.

REFLECTION: The psalm celebrates victory despite adversity, not freedom from adversity. The Lord could not deliver David from danger unless David had in fact faced real danger. The psalm also takes the long view, not asserting an absence of any individual setbacks, but viewing the bigger picture of God's program of victory for the Davidic heir and the extension of that blessing to those faithful to him.

Psalm 19

THEME: Psalm 19 models the proper human response to the revelation of God and his standards.

TYPE: Mixed: hymn of praise, instruction.

AUTHOR: A psalm (*mizmor*) of David. For the director of music.

STRUCTURE: This psalm has three stanzas of six lines each. Stanzas 1 and 3 consist of four two-part lines (bicola) plus two three-part lines (tricola). Stanza 2 consists of six short bicola, which in the original Hebrew are each three words plus two words.

Stanza 1 (vv. 1–6) marvels at the testimony of creation. Stanza 2 (vv. 7–9) marvels at the quality of God's revealed will. Stanza 3 (vv. 10–14) expresses the value placed on God's Word and the desire to live acceptably before him.

SPECIAL NOTES: The Lord's name occurs precisely seven times.

David Beach

REFLECTION: Surely the heavens and the sun are radiant and enduring. But these descriptions are said of God's laws. The heavens and sun give witness about God's grandeur, generating awe. His Word is the specific expression of his thoughts, giving the light of wisdom and discernment, a reliable treasure for the soul surpassing mere wealth.

Psalm 20

THEME: May the Lord save the king and grant him victory; our hope is in the Lord not in the means of war.

TYPE: Royal. A prayer for the king.

AUTHOR: A psalm (*mizmor*) of David. For the director of music.

BACKGROUND: The psalm was probably used ceremonially prior to the king taking his armies into battle.

STRUCTURE: The first half of the psalm (vv. 1–5) is prayers of the people on behalf of the king, leading to a statement of confidence that the king will be victorious. Verse 5c concludes the petition and may be considered the center line of the poem. There are two speakers in the second half. In verse 6 a prophetic or priestly voice proclaims confidence that the Lord will save the king. Then the whole community follows with a statement of confidence in verses 7–8, leading to a final line of petition for the king in verse 9.

SPECIAL NOTES: Second Chronicles 20 gives an account of King Jehoshaphat asking God for help facing large approaching armies, and the Lord responds with a prophetic message.

AP/Wide World Photos

REFLECTION: In this plea for victory, three times the psalmist mentions the name of God, each time heightening his relationship to him: the God of Jacob (v. 1), our God (v. 5), and finally the Lord our God (v. 7). Solomon, in his prayer of dedication of the temple in 1 Kings 8, includes, "When your people go to war against their enemies, wherever you send them, and when they pray to the LORD toward the city you have chosen and the temple I have built for your Name, then hear from heaven their prayer and their plea, and uphold their cause" (vv. 44–45).

Jesus is building his followers into a temple made of living stones, and he gives us his name. Consider the power of praying that Jesus mentions in John 14:13: "I will do whatever you ask in my name so that the Father may be glorified in the Son." How often when we pray do we consider his cause? Where is his name at stake in our lives? If only the current of our whole being were oriented toward the victories of Jesus our King. May we clap our hands and shout in a chorus of joy over the triumphs of his cause.

Psalm 21

THEME: The people celebrate God aiding the king against his foes and are assured of the Lord's continued help.

TYPE: Royal.

AUTHOR: A psalm (*mizmor*) of David. For the director of music.

BACKGROUND: The psalm was probably used ceremonially prior to the king taking his armies into battle but may also have been used upon his successful return.

STRUCTURE: The psalm divides into halves of seven lines each. The speaker in the first six lines addresses the Lord directly, praising him for giving the king success. Verse 7 is a proclamation in the third person that affirms the king's trust in the Lord. In the next six lines (vv. 8–12), the speaker addresses the king directly, assuring him of success against his enemies. In the seventh line of the second half (v. 13), he praises the Lord.

Library of Congress, lambdc 08771

SPECIAL NOTES: The request for life in 21:4 recalls the wording of 2:8, though there the request is for defeating foes. The Lord's anger terrifies the king's enemies in 2:5, 12 and 21:9. They are in danger of perishing in 2:12 and 21:10.

REFLECTION: Joyous victories, requests granted, rich blessings, a crown of pure gold, splendor, majesty—all of these are pictures of lavish blessings from the Lord. All these move the psalmist to the central proclamation of trust, not in horses and skill in battle, but in the unfailing love of the Most High. Victory is sure when he shows up for battle; enemies flee when he draws his bow. Victories granted to the king are pictures in miniature of his strength and his might. The psalmist exalts the Lord for his strength and sings of his might.

All of our successes and human glory are merely a finger pointing to a far greater hand—a hand that will one day lay hold of all God's enemies. His right hand will seize them. And then all of the redeemed will join in one grand chorus and follow the lead of this psalmist, exalting the Lord and singing of and praising his might.

Psalm 22

© William D. Mounce

THEME: Distressed by enemies and feeling forsaken by God, the psalmist remembers past deliverance and is confident of praising God again in the community of worshipers.

TYPE: Individual lament, royal.

AUTHOR: A psalm (*mizmor*) of David. For the director of music. To the tune of "The Doe of the Morning."

BACKGROUND: The psalmist is severely threatened by enemies.

STRUCTURE: The psalm divides roughly into thirds: verses 1–11, 12–21, and 22–31.

The first major section alternates complaint and lament (vv. 1–2 and 6–8) with motivation for God to respond (vv. 3–5 and 9–10), culminating in a petition for God not to be far off. The motivation is God's past relationship with the psalmist's ancestors and with the psalmist.

The second major section alternates accusations against enemies (vv. 12–13 and 16–18) with lament (vv. 14–15), again culminating in petition for God not to be far off (vv. 19–21). The petitions for God not to be far off reflect David's opening lament asking why God has forsaken him.

The third major section changes tone to confidence. The psalmist's own vow to praise (v. 22) is followed by a call to the Lord's worshipers and motivation to praise (vv. 23–24). The psalm concludes with statements of confidence that the psalmist will be able to fulfill the vow in the assembly of worshipers and the Lord's rule will be evident (vv. 25–31).

SPECIAL NOTES: Jesus quotes Psalm 22:1 (implying, if not reciting, the whole psalm) on the cross. The gospel writers seem to make a point of comparing their accounts to Psalm 22 by pointing out elements such as the mocking and being surrounded by enemies (Matt. 27:29–31, 39–44; cf. Ps. 22:7, 12–13, 16), the phrase "Let him deliver him" (Matt. 27:43; cf. Ps. 22:8), and testimony from the nations (Matt. 27:54; cf. Ps. 22:27). Additionally the descriptions of personal distress in Psalm 22:14–15 and 17–18 are fitting for reapplication to the crucifixion.

REFLECTION: In the midst of our lives, in the extreme stresses of trauma and tragedy, the psalmist has left us an example to follow. Pray these laments, sing these kinds of songs from the depths of your soul to the only one who can save. David is here showing faith in extreme distress, clinging to a simple truth he had learned in the first psalm: "The Lord watches over the way of the righteous."

With the words of this psalm, Jesus embraces pain and suffering, shame and loss, sadness and abandonment with wide-open eyes of faith; he changes his dialogue and his gaze from horizontal to vertical. And by so doing, he binds his loss to God's promises and transforms his suffering from preposterous waste to a paradoxical wonder—a prerequisite for glory.

"Resurrection" occurs after verse 21, and verse 22 opens with a burst of praise for a deliverance so great that "all the ends of the earth will remember and turn to the Lord" (v. 27). And so it is, and so they have, amen.

Psalm 23

THEME: The Lord provides faithfully in the midst of danger from enemies.

TYPE: Confidence.

AUTHOR: A psalm (*mizmor*) of David.

BACKGROUND: The image of a shepherd was often used of a king in the ancient world.

STRUCTURE: There are four main images in the psalm. In verses 1–3 the Lord is pictured as a shepherd providing safe pasture and water for his sheep. In verse 4 the setting is danger, but the shepherd still protects. In verse 5 the Lord provides bounty with enemies around. In the final picture, goodness is personified as chasing down the psalmist.

SPECIAL NOTES: Psalm 23 is a fitting sequel to Psalm 22, which describes in more detail the idea of being surrounded and threatened by enemies.

© Noel Powell/www.istockphoto.com

REFLECTION: As a postscript to Psalm 22, this psalm is an even more wonderful word picture of the redemption of pain and suffering and the transformation of the suffering one—one who found no rest is restored; quiet waters follow the dust of death; raging bulls and roaring lions are kept at bay while a sumptuous feast is spread; the one with out-of-joint bones on display now has anointing oil dripping down his face; and the one with a thirsty mouth dried up like a potsherd now has a cup running over.

Psalm 24

THEME: The Lord is Creator and King, requiring fidelity of those who would approach him.

TYPE: Liturgy, instruction.

AUTHOR: A Psalm (*mizmor*) of David.

BACKGROUND: Psalm 24 may have been recited as worshipers approached Jerusalem. The middle section is like Psalm 15, with question and answer about those worthy to worship. The last section sounds reminiscent of a ceremony of transporting the ark of the covenant. Such a psalm would have been fitting for the occasion of David bringing the ark to Jerusalem, as described in 2 Samuel 6:12–19.

STRUCTURE: The psalm begins with a proclamation of praise that all the earth is the dominion of the Lord, its creator (vv. 1–2). The next section represents a procession of worshipers. It poses the question of who may approach the Lord (v. 3). The answer affirms the character of the true worshiper (vv. 4–5). Lastly it affirms that those approaching are such people (v. 6). The third and final section calls for the gates to be opened for the Lord, the "King of glory," to enter (vv. 7–10).

SPECIAL NOTES: The question-and-answer motif serves to instruct the members of the community. The technique appears elsewhere (Ex. 13:14; Deut. 6:20; Ps. 15) and was also a regular part of the Passover celebration.

REFLECTION: The psalmist gives worshipers approaching Jerusalem a powerful vision of a city personified, lifting up her head to receive the King of glory—a nation waiting for its anointed, the Messiah. It's as if he were walking among them as they were calling out to the city, "Lift up your heads, you gates; be lifted up, you ancient doors, that the King of glory may come in" (24:7). Today the Messiah calls his church to worship and communion: "Here I am! I stand at the door and knock. If anyone hears my voice and opens the door, I will come in and eat with them, and they with me" (Rev. 3:20).

Psalm 25

THEME: The psalmist prays for guidance, forgiveness, and protection.

TYPE: Individual lament, liturgy.

AUTHOR: Of David.

BACKGROUND: The liturgical element is seen in the middle eight lines (vv. 8–15). A prophetic or priestly voice speaks for three lines followed by the psalmist for one line. Then the cycle repeats. That the final line of the poem is a prayer for the nation may indicate the other speaking voice again, but more likely the king has been speaking in the first person and now connects God's treatment of himself as King with the good fortune of the nation.

STRUCTURE: The psalm divides approximately into thirds: verses 1–7, 8–15, and 16–22.

In the first third the psalmist affirms his trust in the Lord and seeks his guidance.

In the second section, a priestly or prophetic voice describes the Lord's faithful guiding character. Then the psalmist asks for forgiveness. The other voice affirms the instruction and prosperity of God-fearers. Then the psalmist affirms his loyalty to the Lord.

The third section is primarily petition for deliverance and forgiveness, with the final line shifting from the first person to a prayer for Israel as a nation.

SPECIAL NOTES: The psalm is an alphabetic acrostic, with each line beginning with a successive letter of the Hebrew alphabet. The psalm is bracketed by the phrase "hope in you" in verses 3 and 21. The Lord's name occurs ten times in the psalm.

REFLECTION: The psalmist does not approach God on the basis of innocence but still comes with great hopes of being answered. On what basis? Because of God's love. Because of God's name. Because of his confidence in how God responds to those who hope in and fear him. Because he expects his hurts to move God to compassion. And because of his repentance. How does the psalmist demonstrate repentance? Not with great words of sorrow, but with a pursuit of obedience and commitment to receiving the Lord's instruction.

Psalm 26

THEME: The person of integrity prepares for worship.

TYPE: Individual lament, possibly liturgical.

AUTHOR: Of David.

BACKGROUND: Like Psalms 15 and 24, the psalmist makes claims to a life of integrity and looks forward to worship at the temple or tabernacle. But unlike Psalms 15 and 24, Psalm 26 does not make use of the question-and-answer motif. Like a lament, it petitions for deliverance.

STRUCTURE: In the three lines of verses 1–2, the psalmist petitions for vindication and invites the Lord to test him. In verses 3–8 the psalmist makes claims of innocence and profession of loyalty. In the next three lines (vv. 9–11), the psalmist petitions for safety, accuses the enemy, and claims to have walked in innocence. The final verse proclaims confidence and vows to praise God in the worship assembly (v. 12).

Steve Mason/Getty Images

SPECIAL NOTES: Psalm 26 makes several allusions to Psalm 1. The references to walking without blame (vv. 1 and 11), not sitting with the wicked (vv. 4 and 5), and standing on firm ground (v. 12) recall the use of the verbs "walk," "stand," and "sit" in Psalm 1:1.

A blameless life (vv. 1, 11) is also referred to in Psalms 15:2; 84:11; 101:2, 6; and 119:1.

REFLECTION: Here the psalmist approaches God on the basis of innocence. It is a bold basis for petitioning God but is not boasting. It leads rather to praising God. Where the psalmist is confident of doing well, we may reflect on how well we do.

Psalm 27

© Oleg Prikhodko/www.istockphoto.com

THEME: The Lord provides protection, and the psalmist desires to be close to the Lord.

TYPE: Mixed: confidence and lament; royal liturgy.

AUTHOR: Of David.

BACKGROUND: The psalm is a composite with a statement of confidence that speaks of God in the third person and an individual lament that addresses God in the second person. This suggests a liturgical setting in which the king proclaims his confidence in God to the assembly and then turns to God in prayer.

STRUCTURE: Verses 1–6 are a statement of confidence. In verses 1–3 the psalmist expresses confidence in the face of enemies because the Lord is his stronghold. The central line of this section is 4a, emphasizing his utmost desire, which is to dwell with the Lord and in his protection (vv. 4–5). Verse 6 celebrates his victory over his enemies leading to worship.

The lament section (vv. 7–12) is mainly petition but expresses concern about the classic lament categories of enemies, God, and personal distress. The content continues the theme of desiring a close relationship with the Lord.

The psalm closes with a statement of confidence by the psalmist, who is then addressed by a priestly or prophetic voice admonishing him to wait for the Lord.

SPECIAL NOTES: The psalm has exactly twenty-two lines, the same as the number of letters in the Hebrew alphabet. While it is not an alphabetic acrostic, the choice of line number is deliberate and signals the unity of the composition.

REFLECTION: There are many things we may want; many things we may put our energy into pursuing. The psalmist wants "one thing" and knows that in a single-minded pursuit of it comes also needed safety. The confidence that goes with this pursuit is the foundation for getting through troubles.

Psalm 28

THEME: God destroys those who disregard him but hears and protects those who turn to him.

TYPE: Individual lament, royal, liturgy.

AUTHOR: Of David.

BACKGROUND: The bulk of the psalm is a lament, probably spoken by the king. A liturgical setting is indicated by the limitation of first-person speech to the first, second, and fourth stanzas, while stanzas 3 and 5 indicate the voice of another speaker.

STRUCTURE: The psalm has five parts: verses 1–2, 3–4, 5, 6–7, 8–9. Stanza 1 is an initial appeal in which it is clear the psalmist fears for his life. Stanza 2 is a petition not to be judged with the wicked, but that God indeed judge them. Stanza 3 is the central basis for the psalm and may represent a priestly or prophetic voice. It is a statement of confidence that the Lord will destroy those who disregard him. Stanza 4 is an expression of thanks for the Lord's help. Stanza 5 shifts to concern for the community with a statement of confidence in the Lord's protection for his people and the king and a prayer that the people be blessed and governed well.

Todd Bolen/www.BiblePlaces.com

REFLECTION: The psalm mentions one specific evil—talking nice but with intent to harm. Too often we hear of scam artists, dishonest salesmen or repairmen, corrupt politicians, and people who seem interested and helpful who turn out to be gossips or worse. All the more do we value integrity. The petition that their plans be foiled or turned on their own heads is not inherently spiteful; it is a simple plea to the judge for justice.

Psalm 29

THEME: The Lord is powerful, like a great storm, and rules as a king bringing peace.

TYPE: Hymn of praise.

AUTHOR: A psalm (*mizmor*) of David.

BACKGROUND: The word for "flood" occurs only here and in Genesis where it refers to the flood at the time of Noah. The surrounding nations, such as those in the geography mentioned in the psalm, had myths about their gods that included defeating watery chaos and establishing order. Choosing the storm imagery and the concluding picture of the Lord enthroned and providing peace was a way to strongly assert in the ancient culture that the Lord of Israel is the one who truly reigns.

STRUCTURE: Stanza 1 (vv. 1–2) is a call to praise the Lord for his strength. Stanza 2 (vv. 3–9) describes the Lord's power as a mighty storm moving from the Mediterranean inland over the forests of Lebanon. The final stanza (vv. 10–11) exalts the Lord as king and the one who strengthens his people.

SPECIAL NOTES: The Lord's name occurs seven times in the combination "the voice of the LORD." It occurs four times each in stanzas 1 and 3 and ten times in stanza 2.

The reference to his temple and those in it (v. 9) refers to his heavenly temple and the angels, or heavenly beings, also mentioned as the "heavenly beings" in verse 1.

Lebanon extends along the Mediterranean coast to the north of Galilee. The desert of Kadesh is north of Damascus. Sirion may refer to Mount Hermon, near the south of Lebanon.

Digital Stock

REFLECTION: News reports and weather channels have provided many images of powerful storms. They can be frightening to watch, even when simply on a screen during good weather. A storm may unleash more energy than an atomic bomb. In an age when many people lived in tents, great storms were more frightening still. In great storms of shaking thunder and crackling lightning, we catch a small glimpse of God's power.

Psalm 30

THEME: The psalmist praises the Lord for deliverance from death and acknowledges dependence on him.

TYPE: Hymn of thanksgiving.

AUTHOR: A psalm (*mizmor*) of David. A song (*shir*). For the dedication of the temple.

BACKGROUND: David expresses his desire to build a temple for the Lord in 2 Samuel 7. There God reminds him of how he has given him rest from his enemies and promises that one of David's sons will reign after him. That son would build the temple. The Lord would establish his kingdom and be like a father to him, correcting him for his sins but staying faithful in love. Psalm 30 contains several such thoughts.

STRUCTURE: In stanza 1 (vv. 1–3) the psalmist praises the Lord for being rescued from death. In stanza 2 (vv. 4–5) the psalmist calls others to praise God for his enduring favor. Stanza 3 (vv. 6–7) is a testimony that the psalmist's fortunes, good or bad, depend on the Lord. Stanza 4 (vv. 8–10) reports the psalmist's past petition for rescue from death. Stanza 5 (vv. 11–12) recounts that the Lord answered and reversed his fortunes.

SPECIAL NOTES: The Lord's name occurs seven times on its own. It appears twice more in the phrase "LORD my God" (vv. 2, 12), forming a literary bracket around the psalm.

REFLECTION: Remembering past deliverance, the psalmist bursts into rejoicing and a commitment to praise God forever. He goes from weeping, wailing, and sackcloth to rejoicing, dancing, and clothing of joy—all pictures of healing and rescue. The Lord has moved from hiding his face to showing his favor, and for this rescue, this healing, all of the faithful are invited/commanded to sing the praises of the Lord.

This is an appropriate psalm for modern-day Israel—regathered or "resurrected" after centuries of displacement and dispersion. It is also appropriate for the church, a temple of living stones, healed, rescued, and filled to overflowing with gratitude and praise.

Psalm 31

THEME: The psalmist seeks protection and trusts in God.

TYPE: Individual lament, possibly royal.

AUTHOR: A psalm (*mizmor*) of David. For the director of music.

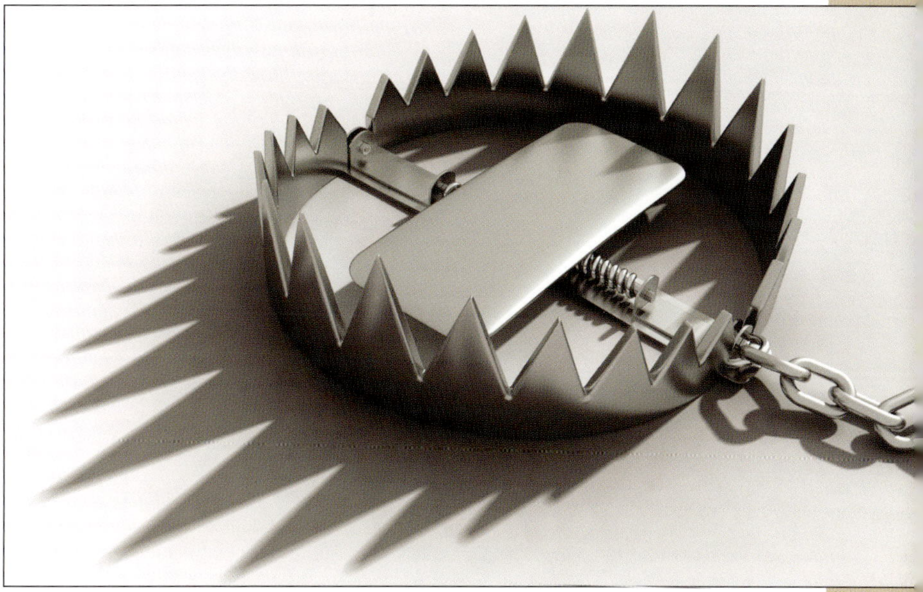

© Mark Evans/www.istockphoto.com

BACKGROUND: Verses 1–20 address God in prayer. It is possibly the king's prayer, made during a difficult crisis that threatened his life and emboldened his foes. Verses 21–24 change to address others, an indicator that they were likely added as a reflection after the Lord delivered the psalmist from the crisis alluded to in the prayer. The psalm portrays the difficulty, tells of the Lord's deliverance, and finally gives an application for the congregation.

STRUCTURE: Statements of confidence are interspersed throughout the stanzas. For the most part, verses 1–5 are a petition for protection. Verses 6–8 are a claim of innocence. Verses 9–13 lament the personal distress and the opposition the psalmist faces. Verses 14–18 are further petition for protection and also judgment on foes. Verses 19–20 express confidence in God's protecting nature.

Then the psalm shifts to address the assembly. Verses 21–22 praise God for answering the psalmist's plea. And verses 23–24 instruct the assembly to love the Lord and wait for him.

SPECIAL NOTES: Jesus quotes Psalm 31:5 on the cross in Luke 23:46. Psalms 31:1–3 and 71:1–3 are nearly identical.

REFLECTION: In reflection on the psalmist's bleak circumstances and deliverance, the final verses instruct us in a response. We should affirm that God preserves the faithful and judges the proud. Therefore, in our difficult circumstances we should love the Lord and keep our hope in him. God's faithfulness is not determined by our current circumstances.

Psalm 32

© juuce/www.istockphoto.com

THEME: Forgiveness is a blessing; uphold the importance of repentance and teachability.

TYPE: Mixed: thanksgiving, instruction.

AUTHOR: Of David. A *maskil.*

BACKGROUND: Standing in the background is the psalmist's past experience of affliction, repentance, and forgiveness reported in a testimony. In addition a prophetic word has been incorporated to invite the attitude of repentance. The psalm begins with the formula "Blessed are . . . ," a wisdom saying that instructs us on the topic to consider and provides the literary framework for the psalm. In this way the psalm is designed to contemplate forgiveness.

STRUCTURE: Verses 1–2 are a wisdom saying. Verses 3–5 are a testimony of the psalmist's experience. Verses 6–7 call for a response from others and state the position of the psalmist. Verses 8–11 are a prophetic voice, first God speaking to the psalmist then the prophet addressing the larger audience.

SPECIAL NOTES: Psalm 1 begins with a similar formula, as do Psalms 41, 106, 112, 119, and 128. These all emphasize righteous living. Psalms 1 and 32 both end with specific reference to the righteous.

The term *maskil* in the title may mean either "skillful," which would be a reference to musical performance, or "making prudent," which would invite the reader to contemplation.

REFLECTION: When do you most feel the blessing that is stated in verses 1–2 (cf. Luke 7:40–43)? How do you think the attitude in the last line of verse 2 relates to being such a blessed person? Verses 3a and 5a present a contrast. Can you think of a story (yours, biblical, or otherwise) that illustrates the events and transition reported in verses 3–5? Beyond the fact of praying in verse 6, how do verses 3–5 inform our understanding of the way or attitude of this praying? How does the prophetic word in verses 8–9 contribute to our understanding of the attitude in verses 6–7? The closing instruction of verses 10–11 describes two groups, while verses 3–5 presented two conditions for the psalmist. How do these work together to affirm the opening blessing?

Psalm 33

THEME: Our hope belongs in the Lord whose word and plans are sure.

TYPE: Hymn of praise.

AUTHOR: Unknown.

STRUCTURE: The major divisions are in a 3-8-8-3 line pattern. Stanza 1 (vv. 1–3) is a call to praise. Verses 4–11 praise the Lord for the reliability of his Word and rule of the nations. Verses 12–19 begin with a wisdom saying about the privileged position of Israel. The remainder reflects on God's rule, meaning that hope for deliverance, whether from enemies or famine, is best placed in him. The final stanza (vv. 20–22) is a statement of confidence in the Lord.

SPECIAL NOTES: While not an alphabetic acrostic, the psalm has exactly twenty-two lines, the same as the number of letters in the Hebrew alphabet. This line count has been chosen for several psalms.

Todd Bolen/www.BiblePlaces.com

REFLECTION: The Lord is faithful, he loves, he creates, he gathers, he speaks, he plans, he thwarts, he chooses, he sees all humankind. Our part? Singing joyfully, loudly, a new song skillfully played. Hearts rejoicing, eyes turned upward, watching, waiting expectantly, trusting in his holy name and his unfailing love. This is a marvelous picture of joyful praise for a faithful God whose plans stand firm forever!

Psalm 34

© Anup Shah/www.naturepl.com

THEME: The Lord delivers his servants; we are to honor and depend on him.

TYPE: Mixed: praise/thanksgiving, instruction.

AUTHOR: Of David. When he pretended to be insane before Abimelech, who drove him away, and he left.

BACKGROUND: "Abimelech," which means "my father is king," may be a title of the Philistine rulers. The name of the ruler as recorded in 1 Samuel 21:10–15 is Achish. David attempted to flee from Saul and take refuge in Philistia. But the men of Gath (Goliath's hometown) remembered him as a dangerous enemy. In fear, he feigned insanity to escape.

STRUCTURE: Stanza 1 (vv. 1–3) includes a vow to praise and a call to praise. Stanza 2 (vv. 4–7) praises God for his past deliverance. The third stanza (vv. 8–14) includes a wisdom saying and calls the audience to the fear of the Lord. Stanzas 4 and 5 (vv. 15–18 and 19–21) assure the assembly that the Lord attends to the righteous.

Verse 11, the central line of the center stanza, encapsulates the central invitation of the psalm. Verse 22, the last line, delivers the central thesis of the psalm.

SPECIAL NOTES: Psalm 34 is an alphabetic acrostic, each line beginning with the successive letters of the Hebrew alphabet. The alphabet finishes in the second-to-last line, for the second half of verse 5 was used to include one of the letters. The final line brings the tally to twenty-two, the number of letters in the Hebrew alphabet.

The formula "blessed is/are" is combined several times with reference to the righteous: Psalms 1, 32, 33, 34, 112, 146.

REFLECTION: The psalmist tells his story in fairly general terms: he called out, the Lord heard, the Lord delivered. This, he says, is a faithful pattern for all the righteous: they cry out, God hears, God delivers. Always. No one who takes refuge in him will be condemned. "Taste and see for yourself," he says.

A reason to sing indeed.

Psalm 35

THEME: The psalmist implores the Lord to fight on his behalf.

TYPE: Individual lament.

AUTHOR: Of David.

BACKGROUND: Those to whom the psalmist has been good have turned against him and seek his destruction.

STRUCTURE: Stanza 1 (vv. 1–3) is a petition for God to fight on behalf of the psalmist. Stanza 2 (vv. 4–6) is imprecatory, calling for judgment against the enemies. Stanza 3 (vv. 7–10) provides motivation for God to answer. It includes an accusation against the enemies and a vow to praise God. Stanza 4 (vv. 11–16) makes accusations against the enemies and protests the psalmist's innocence. Stanza 5 (vv. 17–21) mixes complaint, accusations, and a vow to praise as further motivation for God to answer. Stanzas 6 and 7 (vv. 22–25 and 26–27) act like stanzas 1 and 2, petitioning God to act and calling for punishments on the enemies. The concluding line is a vow to praise God for when he will have acted.

Jay King

REFLECTION: This may well be called the lament of the mocked and maligned.

The psalm specifically illustrates the general pattern of the previous psalm—the righteous cry out, God hears, God delivers. Invited into the psalmist's present crisis, we hear this warrior's imprecation against "enemies" who were close enough that he grieved for them like a brother. These are not national enemies necessarily, but those who assume the spirit of an enemy: they pursue; they plot; they hide a net and dig a pit; they slander without ceasing; they maliciously mock; they gnash their teeth; they falsely accuse and sneer; and they gloat over his distress.

This is not merely vengeance wresting matters into his own hands; it is a warrior's faith trusting that the faithful and righteous God of Israel, who sees all, will indeed treat his unrighteous enemies like the chaff blowing in the wind of Psalm 1, will confuse and put to shame all who behave in this way, and indeed will deliver those who take refuge in him. Then the delivered one can fulfill his vow to participate in the festivals of praise.

Psalm 36

THEME: The character of the wicked and the character of the Lord are contrasted, leading to a petition to protect the righteous.

TYPE: Individual lament.

AUTHOR: Of David the servant of the LORD. For the director of music.

STRUCTURE: Verses 1–4 are an accusation against enemies. Verses 5–9 praise the Lord and express confidence in his protection. Verses 10–12 are a petition for God to protect the psalmist and for the wicked to fall.

SPECIAL NOTES: Laments are usually classified as an individual or a communal lament. Most of the psalm is not specific either way. Verse 10 seems concerned with the broader community and verse 11 with the individual psalmist. The individual is thus positioned as part of the larger community.

REFLECTION: The psalmist, in the light of God's light, sees a distinction between the sinfulness of the wicked and the righteousness of the upright in heart; he sees the blindness of proud eyes and the plotting in secret. Then in prophetic vision he invites us with him to see the evildoers fallen, thrown down, not able to rise—by faith, the fulfillment of his imprecations in the previous psalm.

Psalm 37

THEME: The wicked are headed for downfall; the Lord watches over the righteous.

TYPE: Wisdom.

AUTHOR: Of David.

© Christopher Logan Slough/www.istockphoto.com

STRUCTURE: Psalm 37 is an alphabetic acrostic, with every other line beginning with the successive letters of the Hebrew alphabet. In the most basic sense it has twenty-two units of two lines (usually two verses in translation). On a larger scale we can suggest four units.

Verses 1–9 contain a series of commands and end with a reference to those who "hope" in the Lord. These verses advise not to worry or to give in to anger but to trust the Lord, who provides for those who do good but cuts off the evil.

Verses 10–20 contrast the outcomes for the wicked and the righteous, but emphasize the downfall of the wicked. Verses 21–33 continue this contrast but emphasize the protection of the righteous and the nature of their good character. The central piece of these verses, verse 27, has the only command in this section and puts in a nutshell its central promise.

Verses 34–40 begin with the admonition to "hope in" the Lord. The Hebrew word for "wait" is the same as the word for "hope," ending the first section in verse 9. This section again contrasts the end results for the righteous and the wicked and has several commands.

SPECIAL NOTES: Beginning in verse 10 the "wicked" are referred to thirteen times and the "righteous" nine times. Recall Psalm 1:6: "For the LORD watches over the way of the righteous, but the way of the wicked will be destroyed." Psalm 37:2 also echoes Psalm 1:3.

REFLECTION: Being still and waiting patiently are acts of faith that can transform impatient anger. With an expectant eye to the future, this elderly psalmist advises us to trust in, delight in, commit our way to, and take refuge in the Lord—each line cascading into the next—ending in stillness and rest. In stillness we can hear the staggering laughter of God as he mocks evil (an echo of Ps. 2). It is in waiting—quieting horse and chariot, muscle and bone, which is often the hardest act of faith—that the meek shall inherit the land (vv. 11, 34).

Psalm 38

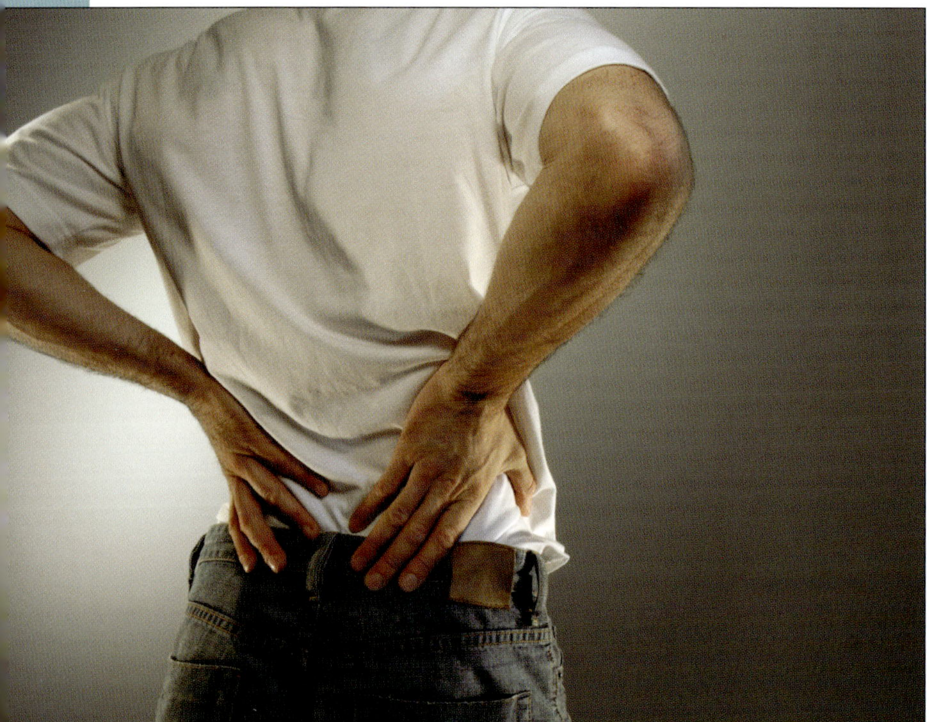

© Pali Rao/www.istockphoto.com

STRUCTURE: The psalm may be divided into five stanzas of four lines each plus a concluding two-line petition. Verses 1–4 are a petition that the Lord not overwhelm the psalmist with anger about sin. Verses 5–8 lament the psalmist's physical distress, while verses 9–12 grieve over broken relationships. Verses 13–16 hint at a struggle with depression but still proclaim confidence in God. Verses 17–20 show the psalmist feeling at the end of a rope, in physical pain, beset by enemies and disturbed by sin. Finally, verses 21–22 petition the Lord not to leave but to come and save.

THEME: When sick, lonely, oppressed, and guilty—then confess, describe woes, and petition for mercy and rescue.

TYPE: Individual lament.

AUTHOR: A psalm (*mizmor*) of David. A petition.

SPECIAL NOTES: While not an alphabetic acrostic, the psalm has exactly twenty-two lines, the same as the number of letters in the Hebrew alphabet. This line count has been chosen for several psalms. Psalm 38:1 closely echoes Psalm 6:1.

REFLECTION: This psalm paints a wonderful verbal picture of confession. The connection between our spirit—the core of our being—and our bodies is far from a recent discovery. A constellation of parallels—anguish of heart, overwhelming guilt and searing pain, etc.—describe "wounds" resulting from sinful folly. Another constellation describes the psalmist's response—"I mourn ... I groan ... I wait ... I confess ... I seek only to do what is good"—a full-orbed, unreserved, holistic participation in confession of sin and petition for deliverance.

Psalm 39

THEME: Life is short; our treasure is in the Lord, not in the hustle and bustle of life or in money.

TYPE: Individual lament.

AUTHOR: A psalm (*mizmor*) of David. For the director of music. For Jeduthun.

BACKGROUND: The troubles of old age prompt the psalmist to reflect on the meaning of life.

STRUCTURE: Stanza 1 (vv. 1–3) reveals a struggle in the heart. The psalmist chooses a course of silence, to say nothing — good or bad — when the wicked are around. The strategy is used to avoid saying anything wrong but creates an inner conflict because of the desire to speak up. In stanza 2 (vv. 4–5) the psalmist speaks, not directly to the wicked, but to the Lord. The wise observation is cast first in personal terms, "my years," then broadens in the last line, "Everyone is but a breath."

The central line, as a wisdom saying, addresses everyone. Verse 6 restates the brevity of life and remarks on the futility of life's hurry and the inadequacy of the pursuit of wealth.

In the next stanza, the psalmist reflects personally and addresses God. Hope belongs only in the Lord. Sin needs forgiveness, and people need for God's wrath to have an endpoint. Again, "everyone is but a breath" (v. 11). The last stanza (vv. 12–13) is a petition. The psalmist asks for relief from God's chastening before death comes.

SPECIAL NOTES: The psalmist's request for God to "look away" in verse 13 is not a request for God to pay no attention. It refers back to the previous stanza and asks God not to attend to punishing him for sins.

PhotoDisc

REFLECTION: The foreigner and stranger theme recalls Abraham, Isaac, and Jacob as strangers and foreigners to whom God was faithful. It also recalls the Year of Jubilee, a reminder that "the land is mine, for you reside in my land as strangers and sojourners" (Lev. 25:23). He is the King, and we are his guests; our hope is in him.

Psalm 40

© Stacey Gamez/www.istockphoto.com

THEME: The king requests deliverance in the future, as in the past, based on pleasing God and being poor and needy.

TYPE: Mixed: royal praise and lament.

AUTHOR: A psalm (*mizmor*) of David. For the director of music.

BACKGROUND: This psalm is for a ceremony involving the king. Though most of the psalm is spoken in the first-person singular, the presence of and concern for the community is indicated by reference to "our," "us," and the "assembly" in verses 3, 5, 9–10 and by referring to people in certain classes (vv. 3, 4, 16).

STRUCTURE: Stanza 1 (vv. 1–3) praises the Lord for deliverance. In stanza 2 (vv. 4–5) the king declares as blessed those who rely on the Lord, and he praises him over false gods. Stanza 3 (vv. 6–8) elevates a proper attitude beyond the making of sacrifices only. Stanza 4 (vv. 9–10) commends declaring the good news of God's works. Stanza 5 (vv. 11–13) petitions the Lord for compassion, despite many sins, and for deliverance. Stanza 6 (vv. 14–17) asks that justice be done to his opponents while those who seek the Lord rejoice. In conclusion (v. 17) the king positions himself among the "poor and needy" as a basis to petition for deliverance.

SPECIAL NOTES: The "scroll" mentioned in verse 7 probably refers to the book of Deuteronomy and in particular to the requirements of the king in chapter 17. The king was to copy and keep God's law (cf. v. 8).

Psalm 70 is nearly identical to Psalm 40:13–17.

REFLECTION: Sometimes, out of impatience, we may ask, "What have you done for me lately?" This question can reveal how quickly some will change allegiance. But the psalmist waited patiently, and the Lord delivered. God's wonders in the past are the assurance to wait patiently for him to act in the future. Take time to recall God's help. And like the psalmist, proclaim it in the assembly. It is a daring but worthy hope when troubles surround.

Psalm 41

THEME: The psalmist testifies to the Lord's deliverance from illness, though foes desired his demise.

TYPE: Mixed: instruction, lament.

AUTHOR: A psalm (*mizmor*) of David. For the director of music.

STRUCTURE: An instructional saying in verses 1–3 acts as an umbrella over a traditional lament in verses 4–13.

Verses 1–3 serve to instruct by beginning with praise to God that came after the deliverance requested in the lament. The psalmist's ordeal recorded in the lament and the deliverance act as proof for the blessing affirmation in the opening verses.

The pattern of the lament in verses 4–13 is initial appeal in verse 4, accusations against enemies in verses 5–9, petition in verse 10, and a statement of confidence in verses 11–13.

SPECIAL NOTES: Psalm 41 ends book 1 of the Psalter. Verse 13 may act as the end to book 1 of the Psalter rather than as the end of the psalm, or it may serve both purposes.

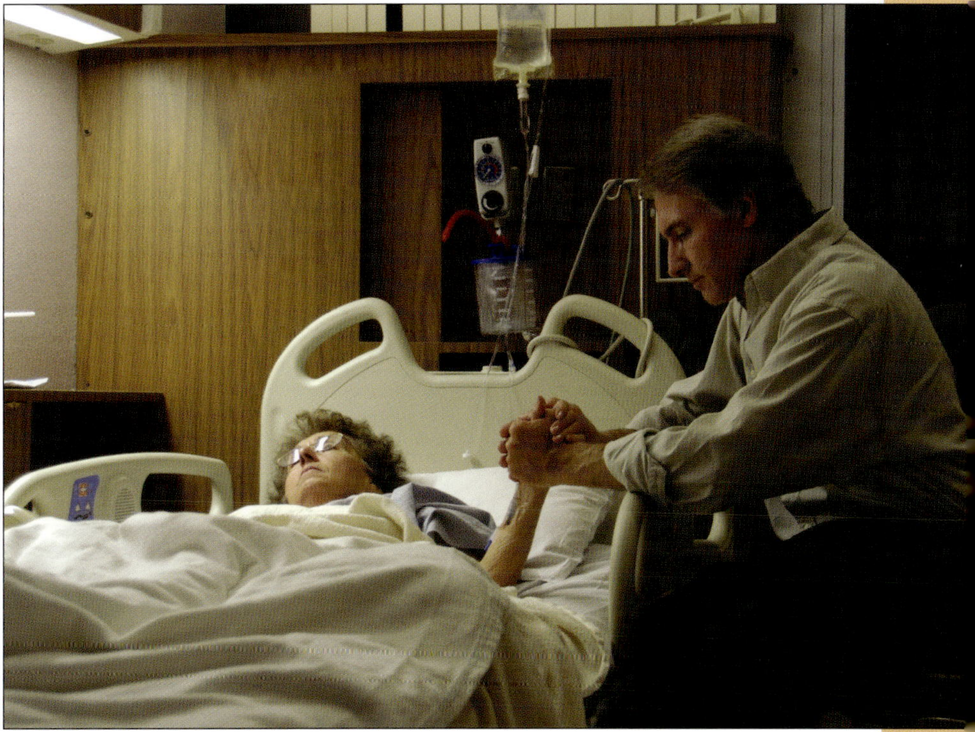

© Claudio Rossol/www.istockphoto.com

REFLECTION: Over half the psalms in the first book of the Psalter are laments. They name many struggles and vary in the basis of their appeal to God. A common thread is expression of confidence in God. Here confidence is further stressed by placing the instructional saying up front. The stress in the lament is still validated, but the entire experience is placed in that 20/20 perspective offered by hindsight. The Lord delivers.

Psalms 42–43

© Amanda Rohde/www.istockphoto.com

STRUCTURE: This psalm is composed of three stanzas, each ending with the same refrain. The first and third stanzas have eight two-part lines (bicola) plus the refrain. The second stanza has one three-part line (tricolon) inserted into the middle of eight two-part lines (bicola) plus the refrain.

Stanza 1 (42:1–5) laments the psalmist's distance from God leading to the determination to remember being close to God in the worship assembly. Stanza 2 (42:6–10) reveals continued tension over the memory and affirmations of God's love and the disheartened feelings of suffering before enemies. Stanza 3 (43:1–4) petitions God to act and vows to praise him as a result.

SPECIAL NOTES: The repetition of the refrain is one of the strong indicators that these two psalms were originally one song.

Psalms 42–43 begin book 2 of the Psalter. Like book 1, book 2 includes many laments and psalms of David.

The term *maskil* in the title may mean either "skillful," which would be a reference to musical performance, or "making prudent," which would invite the reader to contemplation.

THEME: The psalmist struggles to have professed confidence in God take hold in the soul.

TYPE: Individual lament.

AUTHOR: A *maskil* of the Sons of Korah. For the director of music.

REFLECTION: Multiple emotions parade through the psalmist's heart, from current pains to fond memories and the desire for confidence in God to be felt and take hold. The repetition of the refrain, followed by expressions of discouragement, indicates the struggle to come to feel the confidence that is professed and the difficulty in finding resolution. The final refrain ends the psalm but probably does not indicate an end to the psalmist's turmoil. Not only is the refrain repeated, but the whole psalm is fit for repeated use in an ongoing struggle.

Psalm **44**

Werner Forman/Art Resource, NY

THEME: Finding it unbelievable to suffer defeat when they have been faithful, the nation cries out in pain, but they affirm that God is the only one to turn to.

TYPE: Communal lament.

AUTHOR: A *maskil* of the Sons of Korah. For the director of music.

BACKGROUND: God's people have suffered a major defeat in battle but believe that they have been faithful to God.

STRUCTURE: Stanza 1 (vv. 1–3) praises God for delivering the Promised Land to his people. In light of this, stanza 2 (vv. 4–8) professes confidence in God for victory. Stanzas 3 and 4 (vv. 9–12, 13–16) lament that God has not helped their armies and disgraced them. Stanzas 5 and 6 (vv. 17–19, 20–22) protest their innocence. Finally, stanzas 7 and 8 (vv. 23–24, 25–26) petition God to get involved and help.

SPECIAL NOTES: The psalm puts words to the tension of continuing to hold confidence in God while finding the experience of loss incomprehensible. Were they guilty, their defeat would make sense, but they have not turned from him. This inconceivable experience prompts them to language that otherwise seems nonsensical. They ask God why he sleeps. This is common language for the religions of false gods around them but not normally said to the true God (cf. Ps. 121:4).

The term *maskil* in the title may mean either "skillful," which would be a reference to musical performance, or "making prudent," which would invite the reader to contemplation.

REFLECTION: The psalm rings clearly with desperation, but it also contains the echoes of loyalty and confidence. Life doesn't make sense. But that is because we are convinced of God's character and work in the past. And indeed there is nowhere and no one else to turn to. In that disorientation God is both accused and pursued. Be honest with God; he can take it.

Psalm 45

THEME: The people bless the king on the occasion of his wedding.

TYPE: Royal.

AUTHOR: A *maskil* of the Sons of Korah. For the director of music. To the tune of "Lilies." A wedding song.

© DIGIcal/www.istockphoto.com

STRUCTURE: The main portion of the psalm concerns the royal groom and bride. Verses 3–5, an address to the king, are followed by a description of the grandeur of the king in verses 6–9. Then verses 10–12 are an address to the bride followed by a description of the grandeur of the bride in verses 13–15. The second verse and the second to last enclose this section with praise and blessing for the king and his sons. The first and last verses form a literary enclosure in which the poet or singer introduces the wedding song and closes with a promise to continue praising the king.

SPECIAL NOTES: The references to the gold of Ophir, myrrh, aloes, cassia, ivory, and Tyre suggest trade with a variety of places in the ancient world. Tyre is a city on the southern Mediterranean coast of Lebanon, northwest of the Sea of Galilee. It was a port city of Phoenicia that traded around the Mediterranean.

The word "God" in verse 6 is occasionally applied to people of high position and may refer to the king here.

The term *maskil* in the title may mean either "skillful," which would be a reference to musical performance, or "making prudent," which would invite the reader to contemplation.

REFLECTION: Whether royal or common, the bride is beautiful and the groom is grand. Amid royal pomp and circumstance, we see the themes for all marriages that appear in Genesis 1:28 and 2:23–24: leaving parents and joining as one to make a new home and being fruitful and multiplying.

Psalm 46

Copyright 1995–2010 Phoenix Data Systems

THEME: The Lord is our fortress; he will be exalted among the nations.

TYPE: Zion song.

AUTHOR: A song (*shir*) of the Sons of Korah. For the director of music. According to *alamoth*.

BACKGROUND: Zion, another name for Jerusalem, was the capital of Israel under David and Solomon and remained the capital of the southern kingdom of Judah. It was the place God chose to "put his Name" (Deut. 12:21; 26:2; 2 Chron. 6:20). A celebration of Zion is inherently a celebration of God at work, ruling the world.

STRUCTURE: The psalm has three sections of three lines: verses 1–3, 4–6, and 8–10. Verses 7 and 11 are identical and represent a refrain sung by the congregation. Verses 1–3 testify to confidence in God as a refuge. Verses 4–6 sound the praise of Zion, secure because God dwells there. Verses 8–10 invite all to recognize God's power and rule. The refrain affirms that God is with his people.

SPECIAL NOTES: "God" occurs seven times in the psalm, and the Lord's name three times, a total of ten. Compare Psalm 48.

REFLECTION: "Did we in our own strength confide, our striving would be losing." Psalm 46 was inspirational for Martin Luther's hymn "A Mighty Fortress Is Our God." Neither the psalm nor the hymn envisions a lack of battle or a lack of trouble. But both do envision victory. God "makes wars cease" by winning them. His mighty strength is terrifying in its own right, but using that strength makes his people secure. "God's truth abideth still. his kingdom is forever."

Psalm 47

© DNY59/www.istockphoto.com

THEME: The Lord reigns over all nations; praise him.

TYPE: Hymn of praise (celebration of the Lord's kingship).

AUTHOR: A psalm (*mizmor*) of the Sons of Korah. For the director of music.

BACKGROUND: Other nations around Israel are known to have an "enthronement festival." This psalm fits into that cultural setting, picturing God ascending the throne. Public ceremony using the psalm may have included some type of performance representing his taking his heavenly throne.

STRUCTURE: Stanza 1 (vv. 1–4) calls the nations to praise, after which God's people praise him for subduing nations. The central stanza (vv. 5–6) describes God's ascent to the throne and calls for his praise as King. The third stanza (vv. 7–9) affirms his kingship over all nations.

SPECIAL NOTES: The surrounding cultures tended to think of the gods as being in charge of some particular thing, such as rain or crops, or in charge of a place, such as Moab or Edom. In Israel one God rules all places. He is portrayed as the God not of a place but of a people, emphasizing his pursuit of a relationship with humankind.

REFLECTION: Gentiles rejoice that the God of Abraham rules all nations, because that means all may have a relationship with him. Children of faith are the children of Abraham (Gal. 3:7), and through Jesus the "blessing given to Abraham" has come to the Gentiles (Gal. 3:14).

Psalm 48

Danny Frese/www.BiblePlaces.com

THEME: The Lord reigns justly from Zion; we will follow him always.

TYPE: Zion song.

AUTHOR: A psalm (*mizmor*) of the Sons of Korah. A song (*shir*).

STRUCTURE: The flow of thought through the stanzas is as follows: stanza 1 (v. 1), God is great; stanza 2 (vv. 2–3), Zion is his city; stanza 3 (vv. 4–7), advancing kings became afraid there; stanza 4 (v. 8), God keeps Zion secure; stanza 5 (vv. 9–11), the people reflect on the extent and justice of God's rule; stanza 6 (vv. 12–13), an invitation is extended to tour and praise Zion; stanza 7 (v. 14), the people follow Zion's God.

SPECIAL NOTES: There are some word plays in the Hebrew that suggest a movement around the points of the compass in stanzas 2, 3, 5, and 6 from north to east to south to west. As a literary device, this movement underscores the psalm's claim that the Lord rules the whole earth.

"God" occurs eight times in the psalm and the Lord's name two times, a total of ten. Compare Psalm 46.

REFLECTION: God is powerful and dangerous. Therefore his people are safe. God's enemies are shocked. His people rejoice. Verse 8 says "as we have heard, so we have seen." And we consider what we have seen to tell the next generation (v. 13). Are we diligent about telling the next generation of the Lord's provision and protection? Meditate on his unfailing love. What can you say to the next generation?

Psalm 49

© Denis Barbulat/www.istockphoto.com

STRUCTURE: After a four-line introduction, the psalm has two eight-line sections, each followed by nearly identical one-line refrains. The introduction (vv. 1–4) calls the audience to listen. Stanza 2 (vv. 5–11) reflects on the limits of wealth and the certainty of death. Stanza 3 (vv. 14–19) contrasts the fate of the boastful to Sheol, or the realm of the dead, with the psalmist's fate of being rescued from Sheol. It instructs us not to worry about the wealth of others. The refrain (vv. 12 and 20) compares humans to beasts.

THEME: Death takes us all; money brings no privileges.

TYPE: Wisdom.

AUTHOR: A psalm (*mizmor*) of the Sons of Korah. For the director of music.

SPECIAL NOTES: While not an alphabetic acrostic, the psalm has exactly twenty-two lines, the same as the number of letters in the Hebrew alphabet. This line count has been chosen for several psalms.

REFLECTION: You can't take it with you. Many are the biographies of those who had wealth and temporary pleasures, prestige and power, but no peace, no lasting comfort, only a veneer of stimulation over emptiness and anxiety. They ended life with nothing.

The psalm's refrain makes a subtle shift. First it compares humans to beasts in that all die. Then it casts those who have wealth without understanding as being like beasts. The solution is not to be poor in wealth but to be rich in understanding, not trusting in riches one has nor envying riches one does not have.

Psalm 50

THEME: The Lord is a mighty God who judges from and in Zion. Worship with purity; make no pretenses.

TYPE: Mixed: Zion song, instruction.

AUTHOR: A psalm (*mizmor*) of Asaph.

BACKGROUND: The opening summons calls for witnesses as in a court setting where God testifies (v. 7). But the defendants, as it were, are divided into two groups. One group is instructed in the purity of worship; the other is blasted for pretending one thing with what they say while living differently.

STRUCTURE: The line pattern of the stanzas is 7-7-2-7-2 set out as verses 1–6, 7–13, 14–15, 16–21, and 22–23. The opening stanza praises God as a mighty judge in Zion. Stanza 2 addresses Israel, stating that God has no real need of sacrifices, and stanza 3 issues commands that focus on Israel's attitude. In stanza 4 God indicts and shuns the wicked, while stanza 5 issues commands and describes the consequences for dishonoring and honoring God.

SPECIAL NOTES: Psalm 50 shares several characteristics of Zion hymns: it declares that God is mighty and that he rules from Zion and executes justice. Here, however, he addresses Israel rather than defending her from other nations.

REFLECTION: Having a position of privilege does not mean having no accountability. God has chosen Israel and Jerusalem and has ordained worship there. What a privilege! But merely going through the motions misses the heart of the relationship. Making sacrifices is worthless if you act without integrity. Quoting Scripture is merely making sound waves if you join with sinners. And following the crowd, thinking you can get away with cutting others down, copying those who take what isn't theirs, hanging out with those seeking immoral stimulation, and trying to deceive and hide wrong behavior will not be without consequences. God will call all of us to account.

Psalm 51

© Aldo Murillo/www.istockphoto.com

THEME: The psalmist takes ownership of sinfulness and sinful choices and appeals for cleansing and mercy.

TYPE: Individual lament, royal.

AUTHOR: A psalm (*mizmor*) of David. For the director of music. When the prophet Nathan came to him after David had committed adultery with Bathsheba.

BACKGROUND: The story of David's adultery, Nathan's dramatic confrontation, and David's subsequent contrition as told in 2 Samuel 11 and 12.

STRUCTURE: Stanza 1 (vv. 1–2) is a petition for mercy and forgiveness. Stanza 2 (vv. 3–6) is a confession of sin. Stanzas 3 and 4 (vv. 7–9 and 10–12) are petitions for forgiveness, cleansing, and restoration. Stanza 5 (vv. 13–17) begins with a vow to teach others to repent, which is followed by petitions and motivation for God to answer. The last stanza is a prayer to prosper Zion.

SPECIAL NOTES: "Salvation" in verse 12 does not refer to the New Testament sense of the word, and taking away the Holy Spirit in verse 11 does not refer to loss of salvation. After Saul's presumptive sins, God rejected him from being king (1 Sam 13:13–14; 15:26). Part of this consequence was that God removed his Spirit from Saul—that is, he no longer assisted Saul in the role of king and instead sent an afflicting spirit, or angel, to trouble him (1 Sam 16:14). As God is "with" people in the tasks that he assigns, God also "leaves" people in the sense of no longer helping them in a task. David is concerned about losing office in a similar way to Saul.

REFLECTION: Why does verse 16 say that God does not delight in sacrifice, while verse 19 indicates that he does? Torah, the Law, did not describe sacrifices for intentional and presumptuous sins like David's. Sacrifices do not "pay" for sins. There is no possibility of presuming that having a certain amount of cattle to sacrifice later will justify a purposeful sin. Such sacrifices will not be accepted (cf. Prov. 15:8). For a deliberate sin, David can only appeal for mercy with the essence of sacrifice, the true repentance of a broken and contrite heart. After this is resolved, God will again take delight in properly offered sacrifices. The danger of being certain of forgiveness is presuming upon it and failing to be broken.

Psalm 52

THEME: Human treachery will not outdo the Lord's faithfulness to those who trust in him.

TYPE: Mixed: confidence, instruction.

AUTHOR: A *maskil* of David. For the director of music. When Doeg the Edomite had gone to Saul and told him: "David has gone to the house of Ahimelek."

BACKGROUND: At Jonathan's warning of threat to his life, David fled from Saul. First he stopped in Nob and visited the priest Ahimelek, who gave him bread and the sword of Goliath (1 Sam 21:1–10). Then he tried to flee to Philistia (Ps. 34) and eventually to Moab (1 Sam. 22:3). Doeg the Edomite reported Ahimelek's help to Saul, who then ordered Doeg to kill the priests. David felt responsible for the priests' deaths (1 Sam. 22:22).

STRUCTURE: The psalm has three stanzas of four lines each. Stanza 1 (vv. 1–4) begins with a rhetorical question to highlight underlying values and proceeds as an accusation against the wicked. Stanza 2 (vv. 5–7) expresses confidence that God will act against the wicked, which will serve to instruct the righteous. The third stanza (vv. 8–9) is a personal statement of confidence.

SPECIAL NOTES: The term *maskil* in the title may mean either "skillful," which would be a reference to musical performance, or "making prudent," which would invite the reader to contemplation.

REFLECTION: Echoes of Psalms 1 and 2 resound as the psalmist indicts those "who practice deceit" and whose "tongue plots destruction." He imagines righteous witnesses observing the future ruin of this lover of evil—and laughing. God's laughter, heard also in Psalm 2, echoes here from the throats of victims as their perpetrator is "snatched up," "plucked from his tent," and "uprooted from the land of the living"—the destroyer destroyed—analogous to the wicked in Psalm 1.

The psalmist, by contrast, flourishes like an olive tree. The object of his trust, unlike the destroyer who trusts in wealth, is God's covenant love; the object of his hope is God's name. (Because of God's love and goodness, David prays for judgment on the manic anger of Saul, who through Doeg, the violent swordsman, killed the whole town of Nob. How loving and good God's justice would be also for Abiathar, the lone survivor, anguished and aggrieved after losing his whole family and all of his townspeople.)

However difficult it is for us to reconcile God's love with his judgment, they are here juxtaposed—his love serving as a basis for confidence in future judgment.

Psalm 53

THEME: Fools, in their ignorance, may seem to succeed; but they will be judged.

TYPE: Mixed: instruction, lament.

AUTHOR: A *maskil* of David. For the director of music. According to *mahalath*.

BACKGROUND: The psalm offers insight on the problem of wicked people who have success for a time.

Concerning its type, the psalm is like a court scene in which the fool is indicted and sentenced. The psalmist offers the Lord's perspective as he observes evildoers, similar to prophetic instruction. But the psalm also has elements similar to a lament. For example, the indictments are like the accusations of a lament. It also has a statement of confidence. And like many laments, it ends with a petition for God to save.

Todd Bolen/www.BiblePlaces.com

STRUCTURE: Psalm 53 has four stanzas with verse 4a as the central line. Stanza 1 (v. 1) expresses the perspective of the fool. Stanza 2 (vv. 2–3) gives God's perspective and indictment of human corruption. As a rhetorical question, the central line expresses a central thought—that evildoers are clueless. The third stanza (vv. 4–5) gives an indictment and proclaims the punishment of the wicked. The final stanza (v. 6) is a petition for God to act from Zion to restore his people.

SPECIAL NOTES: The meaning of *mahalath* in the title is uncertain but may relate to entreating. It occurs only here and in Psalm 88, which is a desperate prayer.

The "fool" is a fool in the area of morality; the term has nothing to do with skills, aptitudes, or intellectual ability.

The term *maskil* in the title may mean either "skillful," which would be a reference to musical performance, or "making prudent," which would invite the reader to contemplation.

Psalms 14 and 53 are nearly identical.

REFLECTION: This poetry invites us to join those who laugh and those who trust; it invites us to entrust all those who are victims of violence to a loving God whose name is good—to let vengeance be his. And it invites us to flourish as persons like olive trees. This psalm is nearly identical to Psalm 14—a description of fools and evildoers who threaten the poor and devour God's people as they would devour bread. In Psalm 14 the righteous declare the Lord as their refuge.

This psalm rolls out the same scenery, but in the third stanza we hear the voice of the scop (schope), an ancient term for a war correspondent—one who studies and describes the battlefield—reporting back the results to the commander/king. Here the report is total victory. "God scattered the bones" of the attackers, for "God despised them" (v. 5). Those who placed their hope and trust in the Lord as their refuge were gloriously delivered. "Let Jacob rejoice and Israel be glad!" (v. 6).

Psalm 54

THEME: Let those who do not regard God have their evil come back on them; but the Lord is the psalmist's sustainer.

TYPE: Individual lament.

AUTHOR: A *maskil* of David. For the director of music. With stringed instruments. When the Ziphites had gone to Saul and said, "Is not David hiding among us?"

BACKGROUND: The Ziphites informed Saul of David's location on two occasions (1 Sam. 23:19; 26:1). In the first case, Saul had nearly surrounded David and his men, a lamentable situation indeed. But Saul had to temporarily leave the pursuit to attend to an attack by the Philistines. Later, and in both of the chases prompted by the Ziphites, David had prime opportunity to take Saul's life but refused (1 Sam 24:6; 26:9). The imprecation in the psalm is reflected in 1 Samuel 24:9–15 and 26:10, 19.

STRUCTURE: The stanzas of the psalm are short and symmetrical in their line structure as: 2-1-1-1-2. Stanza 1 (vv. 1–2) is an initial appeal to be heard. Stanza 2 (v. 3) is an accusation against the enemies. Stanza 3 (v. 4) is a statement of confidence. Stanza 4 (v. 5) is an imprecation. Stanza 5 (vv. 6–7) is a vow to praise and a statement of praise.

SPECIAL NOTES: The imprecation is not a call for malicious cruelty but a call for poetic justice, that the wicked be caught in their own designs.

The term *maskil* in the title may mean either "skillful," which would be a reference to musical performance, or "making prudent," which would invite the reader to contemplation.

REFLECTION: The cry "Vindicate me" occurs six times in the Psalms and once in the backstory of this psalm, 1 Samuel 24:15. The backstory records a conversation between David and Saul, "May he [the LORD] vindicate me by delivering me from your hand." This psalm poetically recounts David's vindication, his deliverance. His cry opens the story and equates vindication and salvation; his praise concludes the story. Salvation, as seen here, vindicates the name, the work, and the character of the yet-to-be-crowned king-select. This picture of salvation invites us to stand with our king-select, join him in his cry for vindication, and celebrate his reign. Each deliverance, each rescue, also invites us to envision final vindication when with the psalmist we can say to the LORD, "You have delivered me from all my troubles."

Psalm 55

J. Haradine

THEME: Dismayed by betrayal and wishing to get away, the psalmist trusts God for safety and leaves justice to God's work.

TYPE: Individual lament.

AUTHOR: A *maskil* of David. For the director of music. With stringed instruments.

BACKGROUND: The background is not certain; however, nearby psalms refer to David on the run from Saul (cf. vv. 6–7). The arrangement invites us to consider the stories of 1 Samuel 23–26 as illustrative of the material in the psalm. The psalm's reference to betrayal by a companion, rather than attacks from an enemy (vv. 12–13), and the broken promises (v. 21) are certainly compatible with this background.

STRUCTURE: The first stanza (vv. 1–3) is an initial appeal with motivation for God to answer. After this, the psalm divides into halves of thirteen lines each in a repeating pattern: 5-3-4-1 and 5-3-4-1. Stanza 2 (vv. 4–8) laments personal distress. Stanza 3 (vv. 9–11) petitions God and gives motivation to answer. Stanza 4 (vv. 12–14) is an accusation expressing feelings of betrayal. Stanza 5 (v. 15) is an imprecation requesting judgment against the enemies. Stanza 6 (vv. 16–19) is a statement of confidence. Stanza 7 (vv. 20–21) is another accusation against the companion who has become an enemy. Stanza 8 (vv. 22–23) gives instruction from a prophetic or priestly voice to trust God. In the final stanza, the last line of verse 23, the speaker is again the psalmist who proclaims trust in God.

SPECIAL NOTES: The term *maskil* in the title may mean either "skillful," which would be a reference to musical performance, or "making prudent," which would invite the reader to contemplation.

REFLECTION: In this psalm the psalmist experiences dark emotions without immediate resolution. He speaks of intense, overwhelming feelings caused by things and people he cannot control or change. Trust—the bedrock of social relations—crumbles in a violent soul-felt tremor of betrayal and broken vows. And the trouble doesn't stop there. Add to betrayal, slander—angry, hate-filled, and deceitful words. Augustine comments that as we listen to the psalmist and acknowledge ourselves to be in the same place, experiencing similar tribulations, we can share in his prayer.† All around us we see broken vows, broken marriages, broken families, broken contracts, and broken treaties. And we can hear this psalm as a courageous prayer for our day, a cry for God to act: "Lord, bring down the wicked and save us."

†Augustine, *Exposition on the Book of Psalms*, in *Nicene and Post-Nicene Fathers* (V1–08), 380.

Psalm 56

THEME: The psalmist trusts God despite slanderous attacks.

TYPE: Individual lament.

AUTHOR: A *miktam* of David. For the director of music. To the tune of "A Dove on Distant Oaks." When the Philistines had seized him in Gath.

© fotostorm/www.BigStockPhoto.com

BACKGROUND: David fled to Gath twice (1 Sam. 21:10; 27:4). The first time turned out to be perilous for David, so he feigned madness to be able to escape. The second time he became a trusted subordinate of Achish; however, when the Philistines went to attack Saul, they distrusted David and opposed him before Achish.

STRUCTURE: Stanza 1 (vv. 1–2) begins with an appeal for mercy and then makes accusations against the enemy. Stanza 2 (vv. 3–4) states the psalmist's confidence in God in the face of mere mortals. Stanza 3 (vv. 5–7) returns to accusations against the enemy and a petition to bring them down. Stanza 4 (vv. 8–9) petitions God to take account of the lament so that the enemy will be turned back. Stanza 5 (vv. 10–11) mirrors stanza 2 as another statement of confidence, trusting God in the face of mere mortals. And stanza 6 (vv. 12–13) expresses the psalmist's vows and praise.

REFLECTION: How often does some form of fear dominate our inner conversations? What if alongside our fears and tears we placed a declaration of trust—trust in a God who gathers our tears and records them? What if we stood in that declaration instead of in our fear of an uncertain future?

Psalm 57

THEME: The psalmist confidently trusts God, but his opponents are caught by their own devices.

TYPE: Individual lament.

AUTHOR: A *miktam* of David. For the director of music. To the tune of "Do Not Destroy." When he had fled from Saul into the cave.

BACKGROUND: In 1 Samuel 24 we read that David and his men hid from Saul in a cave. Saul chanced to enter the same cave to relieve himself, thinking he would have some privacy. David's men wanted Saul dead, but David would not take advantage of the opportunity to kill him. Instead, he secretly cut off a section of Saul's garment. After Saul finished his business and left the cave, David went out and confronted Saul with this evidence of his mercy.

© Bruce Davidson/www.naturepl.com

STRUCTURE: Each half of the psalm ends with the same single-line refrain. In stanza 1 (v. 1) the psalmist appeals to God for mercy based on his trust in God. Stanza 2 (vv. 2–3) continues the thought as a statement of confidence. Stanza 3 (v. 4) laments David's distress of being threatened by enemies. Verse 5 is a refrain of praise. The next three stanzas are an accusation against the enemies (v. 6), a statement of confidence (vv. 7–8), and a vow to praise (vv. 9–10). Finally, verse 11 repeats the refrain of praise.

SPECIAL NOTES: Psalm 108:1–5 repeats Psalm 57:7–11. Such sharing of verses between psalms is evidence that psalm material could be adapted beyond its original setting.

REFLECTION: This psalm gives a rich verbal picture of the psalmist taking refuge in God during a disaster: crying out in the midst of lions—ravenous beasts that spread a net for his feet—and exalting God. The second half, a retrospective, describes the psalmist's deliverance. Aware of and able to name his intense emotions of distress, he sees his enemies fall into the pit they dug for him. His heart, once distressed, he now describes as "steadfast," and he commits to awakening the dawn with singing and with praise for God's merciful love and faithfulness. This psalm is also a picture of life: a mixture of distresses and deliverances—crying out and taking refuge, followed by joyful and exuberant praise that awakens the dawn. And above it all, God is exalted, his glory over all the earth.

Psalm 58

THEME: In an arena of intentional, cruel evil, God is called upon to return justice in like manner, thus vindicating the righteous.

TYPE: Mixed: instruction, communal lament.

PhotoDisc

AUTHOR: A *miktam* of David. For the director of music. To the tune of "Do Not Destroy."

BACKGROUND: The psalm is set up similar to a court case. Since the offense is injustice at a societal level, it is like a communal lament. But as a court case, it has a prophetic or instructional tone.

STRUCTURE: Stanza 1 (vv. 1–2) directly accuses a group of being unjust. Stanza 2 (vv. 3–5) is a general condemnation of the wicked but does not address them directly as in stanza 1. Stanza 3 (vv. 6–8) requests their punishment (an imprecation). Stanza 4 (vv. 9–11) confidently asserts that the wicked will be done away with, which in turn will teach the people that God does indeed judge.

SPECIAL NOTES: The strong imagery of the request for punishment matches the intensity of the wickedness for which they are condemned.

© ericsphotography/www.istockphoto.com

REFLECTION: Like a musical drama, this psalm is rich in verbal pictures of the wicked. We need only look to the horrors of the last century and imagine the murderous cruelties of evil rulers like Hitler, Stalin, Amin, and Pol Pot to understand the sentiments of this psalm—"the righteous will be glad when they are avenged" (v. 10). This is similar to the cry of the saints in heaven for vengeance in Revelation 6:10 and the roar of the great heavenly multitude in Revelation 19:2–3: "'He has avenged on her [the false religious system] the blood of his servants.' And again they shouted: 'Hallelujah!'" Heaven rejoices when one sinner comes to repentance; and heaven also rejoices when violent and murderous men, deaf to the cries of the innocent, are brought to justice. "Surely there is a God who judges the earth." These words are truly a comfort.

Psalm 59

© Yuriy Zelenenkyy/www.istockphoto.com

THEME: The psalmist requests safety from opponents who attack unjustly.

TYPE: Individual lament.

AUTHOR: A *miktam* of David. For the director of music. To the tune of "Do Not Destroy." When Saul had sent men to watch David's house in order to kill him.

BACKGROUND: After a failed attempt to kill David with a spear, Saul sent messengers to David's house for overnight surveillance, intending to kill him in the morning. But David's wife, Saul's daughter Michal, aided in his escape (1 Sam. 19).

STRUCTURE: The psalm divides into equal halves of nine lines plus the refrain in each half. The first half alternates petitioning God to deliver (vv. 1–2 and 4b–5) with accusations against the enemies (vv. 3–4a and 6–7). It finishes with a statement of confidence (v. 8) before the refrain (v. 9), which also proclaims confidence in God.

The second half begins with a statement of confidence (v. 10). Then the psalmist returns to petitioning God to punish his enemies as an object lesson for the world (vv. 11–13). Next the psalmist accuses the enemies (vv. 14–15), which includes a repetition of verse 6. The second half of the psalm also ends with a statement of confidence (v. 16) prior to the repetition of the refrain in verse 17.

SPECIAL NOTES: The verb for "protect" in verse 1b is based on the same Hebrew root as "fortress" in verses 9 and 16.

REFLECTION: In this lament the wicked snarl and howl, God laughs, and the psalmist sings. This lament psalm is also an "imprecatory" psalm—a request for judgment (and here, judgment without mercy). Probably few of us today have prayed this kind of prayer and fewer still have dodged spears or had hit men after them. Even if we had, we may still find it difficult to pray this kind of prayer. But consider the outcome the psalmist desired: to show the authority of God over the nations, that the Israelites would not forget that he is near when they pray, that the world may know that God rules over Israel, and that God's love is seen in his protection. Could it be that our prayers lack this language because we don't take these things as seriously?

Psalm 60

THEME: This psalm expresses struggle and confidence as current military circumstances do not coincide with affirmations of God's commitment and protection.

TYPE: Communal lament.

AUTHOR: A *miktam* of David. For teaching. For the director of music. To the tune of "The Lily of the Covenant." When he fought against Aram Naharaim and Aram Zobah, and when Joab returned and struck down twelve thousand Edomites in the Valley of Salt.

BACKGROUND: The battle mentioned in the title seems to be recounted in 2 Samuel 10 and 1 Chronicles 19. If so, then in view of those passages, the psalm title should perhaps read "Arameans" instead of "Edomites." The two words look nearly identical in Hebrew. The psalm does refer to Edomites (vv. 8–9), so perhaps verses 5–12 were first composed in response to an Edomite threat but used again as fitting the concerns of this occasion as well.

© Rui Pestana/www.istockphoto.com

STRUCTURE: There are three stanzas of four lines each. Stanza 1 (vv. 1–4) mostly complains to God for his rejection and harshness but ends with a contrasting line of confidence. Stanza 2 (vv. 5–8) begins with a petition to rescue and is followed by a prophetic word about God's reign and his favorable treatment of Israel. Stanza 3 (vv. 9–12) mixes complaint, petition, and confidence.

SPECIAL NOTES: Psalm 60:5–12 is the same as Psalm 108:6–13. Such sharing of verses between psalms is evidence that psalm material could be adapted beyond its original setting.

REFLECTION: The psalmist's reality doesn't match the promises of God to aid Israel in battle. Refusing to lie or live in denial, the psalmist exhibits faith longing for evidence. Not with blind faith as an infant, nor with naive faith as a child, but with open-eyed, vigorous-minded, and loyal-hearted faith, the psalmist declares utter dependence on God. Yet God no longer goes out with Israel's armies, and only he can trample down their enemies.

How often do we keenly feel the absence of God's aid, as if our backs are against the wall and our options exhausted? With robust faith we can cry to God, "Save us ... that those you love may be delivered" (v. 5).

Psalm 61

© Terry J. Alcorn/www.istockphoto.com

THEME: The king and the people request refuge and a long reign for the king.

TYPE: Royal.

AUTHOR: Of David. For the director of music. With stringed instruments.

BACKGROUND: The psalm contains many of the elements common to a lament: an appeal to be heard, petition, statement of confidence, and vow to praise. But it lacks any accusation against enemies, complaint against God, or lament over personal distress. So this psalm could be employed in a peacetime ceremony when the king is healthy and God's favor is not in question. The presence of lament components stresses the king's dependency on God.

STRUCTURE: Stanza 1 (v. 1) is an initial appeal by the king for God to hear. Stanza 2 (vv. 2–3) continues this thought on the basis of the king's trust and God's past protection. In stanza 3 (vv. 4–5) the king expresses his desire for refuge and a long reign, a request that is repeated by the people in stanza 4 (vv. 6–7). The king speaks again in the last stanza (v. 8), promising to praise God and keep his vows.

REFLECTION: God's promises create desire. Promises in the Davidic covenant have created deep longings: "I will also give you rest from all your enemies.... My love will never be taken away.... Your kingdom will endure forever before me; your throne will be established forever" (2 Sam. 7:11, 15, 16). This longing is also our longing and our way of life as we await the fullness of time. The promise of rest remains.

Psalm 62

THEME: God is the hope and refuge of the king and the people.

TYPE: Mixed: confidence, instruction, possibly royal.

AUTHOR: A psalm (*mizmor*) of David. For the director of music. For Jeduthun.

BACKGROUND: The psalm is probably royal. Much of the psalm is spoken in the first-person singular. But after the people are admonished to trust God, the assembled community answers, "God is our refuge" in verse 8. There is clearly another voice besides the "I" that is priestly or prophetic, which suggests that the first speaker is the king. Verses 3–4 speak of assaulting and toppling a man, which may represent attacks or rebellions against the king.

STRUCTURE: Stanza 1 (vv. 1–2) proclaims confidence in God. Stanza 2 (vv. 3–4) has two speaking voices. The speaker from the first stanza addresses the enemy directly with accusations. Then another speaker talks not to, but about, the enemy. The enemy talks nice but means harm. The first speaker returns in stanza 3 (vv. 5–6), which is nearly a repeat of stanza 1.

Stanza 4 (vv. 7–8) proclaims the king's confidence in God and advocates that the people trust him. They respond in the affirmative. The prophetic or priestly voice returns in stanza 5. Verses 9–10 instruct not to trust in social position, manipulation, or wealth. The last stanza addresses first the audience (v. 11) and then God (v. 12). It affirms that power really belongs to God, and he metes out justice with integrity.

REFLECTION: The psalmist leads by example. The king's (or leader's) problem is sandwiched between two affirmations of dependence on God. The attacks against him concern the community, and his hope in God should be the community's own. As a leader he does not pretend that there is no opposition; rather, he encloses it in hope and calls the community to that same hope (v. 8). Is their hope in him? No. Social position is nothing (v. 9), and other would-be supports are a waste (v. 10). Power belongs to God (v. 11).

Psalm 63

© Juanmonino/www.istockphoto.com

THEME: Maintain confidence in the Lord's anointed even when things look difficult for that person.

TYPE: Mixed: individual lament and instruction, royal.

AUTHOR: A psalm (*mizmor*) of David. When he was in the Desert of Judah.

BACKGROUND: Second Samuel 15–18 records when David fled from his rebelling son Absalom to the wilderness of Judah. Because the last verse of the psalm refers to David as king, we know that the psalm is not about David's fleeing from King Saul.

STRUCTURE: The psalm has four main elements: three with four lines each, plus the fourth component in the final line. The first element is an appeal that affirms that the psalmist turns earnestly to God. The three lines of verse 1 plus a fourth line in verse 6 give voice to this thought. Though separated by verses 2–5, verses 1 and 6 make up a stanza thematically. The connection between them may also have been made clear in the manner in which the psalm was sung. In stanza 2 (vv. 2–5) the psalmist vows to praise the Lord. In stanza 3 (vv. 7–10) David expresses confidence in God. The fourth component appears in verse 11 as a priestly or prophetic voice instructing the audience to have fidelity to the king.

PhotoDisc

Splitting the first stanza apart puts its fourth line, verse 6, at the center of the psalm and emphasizes the time of the struggle—all through the night. At the same time, its reference to meditating on the Lord is a fitting transition from the lament, thirsting for God, to the statement of confidence, remembering God's help.

SPECIAL NOTES: The king speaks in the first person throughout most of the psalm. The last verse is offset in that it changes to third person, speaking about the king, and is the only three-part line (tricolon) of the psalm. This speaker expresses confidence in the king's secure relationship with God and forecasts the results for those who are loyal to the king (they "swear by God," not another) and those who are disloyal ("liars"). By reference to these conventional speaking activities, the common person is brought into this otherwise royal lament.

REFLECTION: The psalmist identifies his desire for God as thirst—an unfulfilled longing. Jesus also pronounces a blessing for those who hunger and thirst—those who acknowledge an unfulfilled longing for righteousness. Thirst is not popular. We like to be well fed with our thirsts quenched. A condition of thirst runs counter to the expectations of our overfed culture; we typically identify blessing with a lack of hunger or thirst. It is interesting that Jesus, the "bread of life," would bless the hungry and not the well fed. What if approaching God without the unquenchable thirst the psalmist speaks of also means we miss out on the feast of the richest of foods the psalmist names in verse 5? How might such thirst change the way we engage God today?

Psalm 64

THEME: The wicked think they won't be caught, but God brings their own kinds of plans back on their own heads.

TYPE: Individual lament.

AUTHOR: A psalm (*mizmor*) of David. For the director of music.

STRUCTURE: Stanza 1 (v. 1) is an opening appeal for God to listen and protect from the enemy. Stanza 2 (vv. 2–4) is a petition for protection from the wicked, who are described with warlike images. The central stanza (vv. 5–6) accuses the wicked of overconfidence and the belief they will not be held accountable. Stanza 4 (vv. 7–9) is a statement of confidence that God will punish the wicked as a lesson for all humankind. Stanza 5 (v. 10) continues the theme of confidence in God, with the certainty of the righteous rejoicing.

SPECIAL NOTES: Stanza 4 mirrors stanza 2 in its choice of words: "shoot" and "suddenly" (vv. 4 and 7), "their tongues" (vv. 3 and 8), "evildoers" and "works of God" (vv. 2 and 9, where doers and works are based on the same Hebrew root word). The deliberate repetition reinforces the idea that God metes out punishment that fits the evil.

Mark Borisuk/www.BiblePlaces.com

The sentiment of the wicked, that they will not be caught, is similar to those who think there is no God in Psalms 10, 14, and 53.

REFLECTION: This psalm speaks of tongues sharpened like swords and cruel words aimed like deadly arrows shot suddenly without fear, with whispers of sinister encouragement: "Who will see it?" Left unchecked, these weapons destroy the righteous; they destroy reputations and wreak havoc in relationships. Indeed, the human heart and mind are cunning.

But God hears every word. And like Goliath's sword, these words become the weapons of self-destruction. God turns the words, the plans, and the conspiracies back on the wicked—people like Haman and Ahab are ruined.

"All the upright in heart will glory in him" (v. 10)—with words.

"Take up the shield of faith with which you can extinguish all the flaming arrows of the evil one" (Eph. 6:16).

Psalm 65

© Felix Möckel/www.istockphoto.com

THEME: The assembly celebrates its relationship with God, his rule, and his provision.

TYPE: Hymn of praise/thanksgiving.

AUTHOR: A psalm (*mizmor*) of David. A song (*shir*). For the director of music.

BACKGROUND: This hymn of praise shows communal concerns because it is spoken in the first person plural, refers to the peoples, and gives attention to the common agricultural and pastoral economy. It may have been sung in connection with festivals or offerings that celebrated harvest or otherwise expressed gratitude for crops and flocks.

STRUCTURE: Stanza 1 (vv. 1–4) celebrates a close relationship with God at Zion. Stanzas 2 and 3 link God's might over water with his interactions with humanity. In stanza 2 (vv. 5–8) praise of God for his power over chaotic waters flows seamlessly to his power over the peoples, putting all the earth in awe of him. Stanza 3 (vv. 9–13) praises God for sending rain, which stimulates rich growth and provides people with grain.

Todd Bolen/www.BiblePlaces.com

REFLECTION: This psalm paints two big pictures: one of God as the creator and ruler of the earth and nations, and one of God as the ruler of nature and provider. The psalm does not say outright that the Lord is not a stone carving, but it clearly portrays the Lord as the true and living God. What's more, he did not simply wind up the universe and let it go. He answers prayers (v. 2), forgives sins (v. 3), provides true satisfaction (v. 4), and is owed praise and the performance of vows (v. 1).

Psalm **66**

THEME: The community calls people to worship and hear testimonies of God's acts and answers to prayer.

TYPE: Hymn of thanksgiving.

AUTHOR: Unknown. A psalm (*mizmor*). A song (*shir*). For the director of music.

BACKGROUND: In stanzas 2 and 3 the speaker is plural (*we, us, our*), whereas in stanzas 4 and 5 the speaker is singular (*I, me, my*). This structure may envision a public setting that leads to personal testimonies of answered prayer.

© Mary Gascho/www.istockphoto.com

STRUCTURE: Stanzas 1, 2, 3, and 5 begin with a call to praise followed by words of praise. Stanza 1 (vv. 1–4) declares praise for God's character, his might over all peoples. Stanzas 2, 3, and 5 (vv. 5–7, 8–12, and 16–20) describe the praiseworthy acts that God has done. Stanza 4 (vv. 13–15) introduces the individual who has come to fulfill vows to sacrifice to God and praise him. The thought continues into stanza 5 (vv. 16–20), which recounts in general terms that God has answered prayer.

REFLECTION: Two invitations are extended in this psalm. The first is "Come and see what God has done, his awesome deeds for humankind!" (v. 5)—the parting of the Red Sea, the exodus, the conquest. He watches, he rules, he has preserved our lives. The psalmist, rather than feeling lifted up in pride over God's faithfulness to Israel, refers to their history as refinement: "You refined us like silver." Silver requires heat for refinement and is cast many times into the fire. Prison, burdens on their backs, passing through fire and water—the picture painted for us is one of suffering of many kinds, including passing through fire and water, two elements that are necessary for life. This suggests that life itself is testing, refinement.

But the psalm doesn't end there: "You brought us to a place of abundance," a time of rest.

The other invitation extended is "Come and hear … let me tell you what he has done for me" (v. 16). God listened and heard. He has not rejected the psalmist nor withheld his love. "Come let us rejoice in him … Shout for joy to God!"

Suffering, refinement, and rest; distress and lament, deliverance and praise. Life is a mixture of these and a balance.

Psalm 67

THEME: May God's blessing and just rule lead all nations to praise him.

TYPE: Hymn of praise.

AUTHOR: Unknown. A psalm (*mizmor*). A song (*shir*). For the director of music. With stringed instruments.

STRUCTURE: The three stanzas combine petition and praise and, with a mirrored structure, point to the central line of verse 4. Stanza 1 (vv. 1–2) petitions God for blessing so that his saving acts will be famous throughout the nations. Stanza 2 (vv. 3–5) calls the nations to praise God because he rules the peoples well. The assertion of God's rule over all nations is the central line of the psalm. Stanza 3 (vv. 6–7) returns to God's blessing for Israel so that the whole earth will fear God.

SPECIAL NOTES: The Psalms are often concerned with the Lord's name and reputation being known beyond Israel and Judah among the nations. This psalm contains several of the topics related to that theme. The God of Israel relates to or is known to the nations by his saving acts and mighty deeds, by his just rule, and by his blessings on Israel. Other psalms include his protection of Israel.

REFLECTION: Self-interest, mixed motives? It is not wrong to seek a blessing, as the community does in this psalm. But unlike people, God cannot be flattered and buttered up in exchange for favors. This psalm directs the community to greater ends than self-interest. May God bless us—in such a way that he is glorified and praised around the world. May the nations know his equitable rule and guidance and praise him. As God sees our hearts, we must do more than mouth the words; we must put his kingdom first.

Psalm 68

THEME: Israel's God who fights mightily and has taken residence in Jerusalem should be honored and praised by all.

TYPE: Hymn of praise/thanksgiving.

AUTHOR: A psalm (*mizmor*) of David. A song (*shir*). For the director of music.

BACKGROUND: This psalm celebrates military victory. By mentioning Sinai and God's arrival at Zion, it recalls the exodus, the conquest under Joshua, and the security established by David. It would have been fit for festivals related to the exodus or for ceremonies after military victories or for receiving tribute.

STRUCTURE: The beginning of stanza 2 and the end of stanza 9 use similar terms as a call to sing to God and naming God "him who rides on the clouds." The psalm also divides in half, with the second half, stanzas 6 through 10, beginning and ending with the proclamation that God is praised.

Stanzas 1 and 2 (vv. 1–3 and 4–6) petition God to defeat his enemies and call the people to praise the Lord for his justice and aid to the weak. Stanzas 3 and 4 (vv. 7–10 and 11–14) speak of God leading his people to war with great power and defeating kings and their armies. Stanza 5 (vv. 15–18) exalts Zion. Other mountains are jealous of the mountain where God settled.

Todd Bolen/www.BiblePlaces.com

Stanza 6 (vv. 19–23) echoes stanza 1 in portraying God as defeating enemies for the benefit of others. It also ties back to stanza 5 by its specific mention of Bashan. Stanzas 7 and 8 (vv. 24–27 and 28–30) envision God's royal procession to his palace/temple in Jerusalem. The tribes of Israel celebrate while other kings submit. Stanzas 9 and 10 (vv. 31–33 and 34–35) call other nations to give tribute and praise to Israel's God, who empowers his people.

SPECIAL NOTES: The people of Canaan and Phoenicia called their god Baal the "rider of the clouds." Using this title to describe the Lord (v. 4) is a pointed way of saying that Baal is not the one who controls the storm and brings rain.

REFLECTION: An amazing shift occurs in this psalm. The psalmist, in rapt contemplation of the military glory and plundering victories of the Lord, suddenly shifts his focus to the one distinguishing characteristic that sets God above all gods, "Praise be to the Lord, to God our Savior, who daily bears our burdens" (v. 19). This God who shakes the earth when he marches, whose chariots are beyond number, who thunders with a mighty voice, actually stoops to bear the burdens of the lowest of his subjects—the fatherless, the widows, and prisoners. He became flesh and tented among us; he took on himself the iniquities of us all; he was bruised for our sins, and by his wounds we are healed. Truly, "our God is a God who saves; from the Sovereign Lord comes escape from death" (v. 20).

Psalm 69

Stephanie Rausser/Getty Images

THEME: While disgraced and lonely, the psalmist asks God for judgment on enemies and for personal protection so that others will be encouraged.

TYPE: Individual lament.

AUTHOR: Of David. For the director of music. To the tune of "Lilies."

BACKGROUND: Though there are similar themes throughout the psalm, possibly two psalms were combined into one. The first half ends by repeating several words from the first two verses. The second half begins with an appeal for God to answer, a common way to begin a psalm. The final verses indicate that Judah has suffered a military defeat.

STRUCTURE: Psalm 69 has two sets of twenty-two lines (vv. 1–15 and 16–36). Each set has twenty-one two-part lines (bicola) and ends in a three-part line (tricolon).

Verses 1–15. After an initial request for rescue, the bulk of stanza 1 (vv. 1–4) combines the three basic grievances in the Psalms. It laments the distress of being overwhelmed, complains that God has been slow to respond, and makes accusation against enemies while protesting innocence. Verse 5 stands alone, acknowledging that no fault is hidden from God. Stanza 2 (vv. 6–12) bemoans the psalmist's disgrace and loneliness. Stanza 3 (vv. 13–15) asserts confidence in God and petitions for deliverance.

Verses 16–36. The seven lines of stanzas 1 and 2 (vv. 16–18 and 19–21) begin with an appeal to be heard and accusations against the enemies. The next seven lines, which make up stanza 3 (vv. 22–28), call for God's judgment on the enemies. Verse 29 petitions God for protection. And in the last two stanzas (vv. 30–33 and 34–36), the psalmist vows to praise God and calls creation to praise him too.

SPECIAL NOTES: A few psalms are alphabetic acrostics, and several more have twenty-two lines, the same as the number of letters in the Hebrew alphabet.

REFLECTION: How can I describe the indescribable, the overwhelming? One way would be to show it poetically—to take all the letters of the alphabet and place myself in the middle as a picture. In the middle of part 1, shame covers the face of the psalmist. This is a fitting parallel to waters coming up to the neck and to engulfing floods. That these two parts have twenty-two lines, the number of letters in the Hebrew alphabet, but without the acrostic, intensifies the picture—I cannot find the words, I am overwhelmed, and shame covers my face. This is not legitimate shame that leads to repentance, but the wagging enemy fingers of scorn, disgrace, and shame. It is like a pit that I am violently thrown into, that breaks my heart and leaves me helpless. How will I respond? Will I cover myself with the fig leaves of self-contempt or heap contempt on others? The psalmist rejects this shame and appeals to God's love and mercy. He chooses to exalt God's name with this lament, "The Lord hears the needy and does not despise his captive people.... God will save ... and rebuild" (vv. 33, 35). May we also reject this illegitimate shame, and may this be the testimony of our hearts.

Psalm 70

THEME: A request to deliver the king, confound the enemies, and give God's people reason to rejoice.

TYPE: Individual lament, royal.

AUTHOR: Of David. For the director of music. A petition.

STRUCTURE: This psalm has two stanzas of four lines. Verses 1–3 petition God to save the king and to defeat and shame his enemies. Verses 4–5 ask that all who rely on God have reason to rejoice and praise him. But verse 5 contrasts the king who positions himself among the poor and needy and cries out for swift deliverance.

BACKGROUND: Psalm 70 has been excerpted, with minor variations, from Psalm 40 (or perhaps Ps. 70 was a unit added to Ps. 40). Psalm 40 is a royal liturgy in which the king first praises God for past deliverance, then proclaims his fulfillment of the requirements in Deuteronomy 17, and finally appeals to God for future deliverance. This latter appeal is the substance of Psalm 70.

© Anke van Wyk/www.BigStockPhoto.com

REFLECTION: There are two categories of people here besides God and the psalmist: those who seek the psalmist's life, and those who seek God and his saving help. In this age of terrorism, imagining someone governed by a spirit of murder and destruction attacking and doing harm is not difficult. Contrast them with someone who refreshes us, who brings life and blessing. We, like the king in this psalm, are quite needy and fragile—we need people who bring restoration and healing to us. The spirit of mocking, of taking, of murder—diminishes us. But the fellowship of the needy, who also cry out for the king's salvation and the defeat of his foes, will also be the fellowship of those who join him in praising God for his deliverance and help. Do we join in solidarity, as the king does, with the poor and needy? Or do we quickly turn against those who seem weak in order to appear strong?

Psalm 71

THEME: The psalmist pleads for God to stay by him in his old age and promises to praise the Lord to the next generation.

TYPE: Individual lament, possibly royal.

AUTHOR: Unknown. (This is possibly of David, a continuation of Ps. 70.)

BACKGROUND: The psalmist is no longer young, though his age is uncertain. The scenario is that in his old age, opponents threaten to harm him and assert that God has left him. Since the psalmist has been a "portent," or sign, to many people by trusting the Lord, the psalmist likely has some social standing and may even be the king.

STRUCTURE: Stanza 1 (vv. 1–4) petitions God for rescue and protection on the basis in stanza 2 (vv. 5–8) that he has consistently trusted and praised God. Stanza 3 (vv. 9–13) asks God to be near, because his enemies claim that God has abandoned him. Verse 14 is the central line of the poem affirming that the psalmist trusts and praises God. Stanza 4 (vv. 15–18) promises to continue praising God and returns to the petition not to be abandoned during old age. Stanza 5 (vv. 19–21) affirms his confidence in God, leading to the promise to keep praising him in stanza 6 (vv. 22–24).

SPECIAL NOTES: Psalm 71:1–3 and 31:1–3 are nearly identical.

REFLECTION: A key issue is the longevity of God's protection. The psalmist has trusted God in the past. The enemies assert that God has abandoned the psalmist in the present. The psalmist asks for protection to be able to praise God to the next generation. The strength of youth will neither be the salvation of the psalmist nor the measure of the psalmist's value to the next generation. God will be his salvation; the psalmist's wise praise of God will be part of his enduring contribution to the community. After all, utility is not the measure of human worth.

Psalm 72

THEME: May God bless the king with wisdom for governance, prosperity for the nation, and a great reputation with other nations.

TYPE: Royal.

AUTHOR: Of Solomon.

BACKGROUND: When asked to make a request of God, Solomon asked for the wisdom to rule well and quickly gained a reputation for his insight (1 Kings 3; cf. Ps. 72:1–2). His fame was so great that many came to hear his wisdom and see his kingdom, including the queen of Sheba (1 Kings 10; cf. Ps. 72:10).

STRUCTURE: The main body of the psalm is followed by a refrain of praise bringing book 2 of the Psalter to a close. The opening lines (vv. 1–2) ask God to give the king wisdom. His justice then (vv. 3–7) will be like refreshing rain and contribute to the prosperity of the people. His rule will be extensive, and other kings will honor him (vv. 8–11). Verses 12–14 praise the king's just and merciful rule. Verses 15–17a pray for the king to live long and the nation to prosper. The closing line, 17b, confidently declares that the nations are blessed through him.

A poetic refrain and a literary note follow (vv. 18–20). Book 2 of the Psalter is closed with the note in verse 20 that marks the end of this collection of David's prayers. The poetic refrain both closes the collection and ties nicely to the end of the psalm by sharing the international theme of verse 19.

SPECIAL NOTES: The final line of verse 19 echoes the Abrahamic covenant in Genesis 12:1–3 (cf. Gen. 15:18; 17:1–7; 22:18; 26:4; 28:14). The blessing on the son (of the king) brings justice and prosperity to the nation so that other nations give honor to the king and to God.

Masterfile

REFLECTION: Bringing book 2 of the Psalter to a close, this psalm of Solomon works with Psalm 2 sort of like bookends. Psalm 2 informs us of the confidence of God in having established his king, calling all to submit. Psalm 72 asks not simply that the king may live a long life, but that God will grant the king what is needed to rule well. Those who have power to rule have responsibility to adjudicate rightly, to deliver the afflicted, and to rescue the weak and needy from oppression. A just and prosperous rule will bring praise to the Lord God of Israel, and it is one of the ways God will be known beyond the borders of Israel and Judah (cf. Ps. 67).

Psalm 73

Digital Vision/Getty Images

THEME: The wicked may seem to prosper but will be swept away; in contrast God protects the righteous.

TYPE: Wisdom.

AUTHOR: A psalm (*mizmor*) of Asaph.

BACKGROUND: Asaph has observed the wicked prospering, which has created a crisis of faith for him, challenging his belief that God is good.

STRUCTURE: The psalm divides in half both thematically and structurally. The first half has three main sections. Verses 1–3 affirm the principle of God's goodness but contrast this with the prosperity of the wicked. Verses 4–11 lay out specific complaints about the apparent injustice of their situation in life. Their prosperity seems too good to be fair. Verses 12–14 sum up the psalmist's conclusion about the wicked and voice the tempting thought that being good is not worth it.

The second half gives the resolution to the problem in the first half. In verses 15–17 Asaph recognizes that his thoughts were mistaken. This realization has three components. He realizes that the fate of these prosperous wicked is getting swept away (vv. 18–20), that his earlier thoughts had no more perspective than an animal's (vv. 21–22), and that what he does have most essentially is his relationship with God (vv. 23–26). The psalm concludes with a contrast (vv. 27–28) not of prosperity but of fate. The wicked are destroyed, but Asaph has refuge in the Lord.

SPECIAL NOTES: The complaints about the wicked are akin to the material of lament. But initially Asaph held it in rather than turning to God. We hear instead his reflections about trying to deal with the disturbing problem while turned inward instead of toward God.

"My portion"(v. 26). Instead of an allotment of land as its portion, the tribe of Levi received support from the other tribes (Num. 18:6–24; Deut. 18:1; Josh. 18:7). When the Lord took the Levites for his service, thus denying them a portion of land among their brothers, he declared, "I am your share and your inheritance" (Num. 18:20). This psalm uses the language of the "portion" to elevate one's relationship with God to the highest value. Compare Psalms 16:5; 119:57; 142:5.

REFLECTION: Psalm 73 provides a great example of the failure to lament. In laments the psalmists are free to bring God their accusations against their enemies and appeal to him for justice. Asaph, however, turned to negative self-talk for coping with his discouragement and sense of injustice. As a result, he nearly slipped and was "senseless" like a "beast." Eventually he found resolution when he entered the sanctuary, that is, in his encounter with God. But in comparison with the rest of the Psalms, his problem was not so much needing more faith to overcome his problem as it was exercising the faith to bring his problem to God.

Psalm 74

THEME: The people point out the attacks and defiling insults of the enemy and ask God to remember the covenant on their behalf.

TYPE: Communal lament.

AUTHOR: A *maskil* of Asaph.

BACKGROUND: An enemy has successfully attacked Judah and even raided the temple in Jerusalem. The Babylonian attack of 587 BC leading to the exile of the Jews may be the occasion for the psalm, but it may have been written in response to another raid.

STRUCTURE: Eleven poetic lines stand on each side of verse 12, which expresses a central thought of trust in God amid having suffered disaster.

The first half has three stanzas. Stanza 1 (vv. 1–3) asks God why he ignores his people and Zion, where the enemy has wreaked destruction. Stanza 2 (vv. 4–8) describes the actions of God's foes in order to incite God to action. Stanza 3 (vv. 9–11) returns to asking God how long until he acts.

The second half has two stanzas. Stanza 5 (vv. 13–17) praises God for his mighty acts in the past. And finally, stanza 6 (vv. 18–23) calls on God to remember both the enemy's insults and the covenant, so as to act on his people's behalf.

SPECIAL NOTES: The term *maskil* in the title may mean either "skillful," which would be a reference to musical performance, or "making prudent," which would invite the reader to contemplation.

REFLECTION: The recent history of the people contradicts their beliefs from their more distant history. God has acted mightily in the past for his people, establishing his kingship. But currently they are in disaster. This psalm directs their expression of pain and disappointment beyond mere retaliation against the enemy and toward a renewal of their covenant relationship with God. Their interest is not simply relief by any means, but rather, mercy joined to God's cause. The foes mock God himself. The condition of the people and the temple are both bound up with this mocking of the Lord. Their call for deliverance prioritizes his reputation. Their desire to avoid disgrace is not to defend arrogant pride but to identify themselves as the needy who can praise God.

Psalm 75

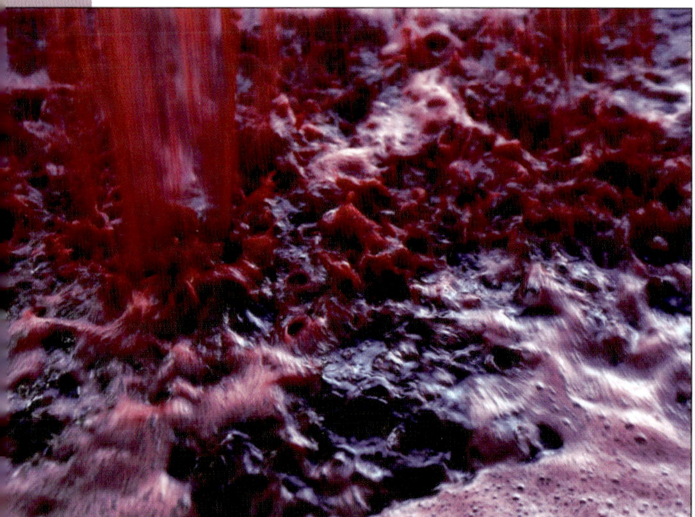

R. Ian Lloyd/Masterfile

THEME: God judges with power and equity; a terror to some, comfort to others.

TYPE: Instruction, possibly royal.

AUTHOR: A psalm (*mizmor*) of Asaph. A song (*shir*). For the director of music. To the tune of "Do Not Destroy."

BACKGROUND: This psalm was probably performed in a service after another psalm of praise. It leads into prophetic instruction rather than words of praise.

STRUCTURE: In stanza 1 (v. 1) the congregation sings of thanks to God. God is the speaker in stanza 2 (vv. 2–5). He asserts his authority and the integrity of his justice and rebukes the boastful. A prophetic or priestly voice speaks in stanza 3 (vv. 6–8), reinforcing God's authority and power and the certainty of judgment. Finally, a single voice speaks in stanza 4 (vv. 9–10). This is likely the king. He vows to praise God and confidently asserts that he will put down the wicked.

SPECIAL NOTES: *Horn.* This imagery of the horn comes from bulls (not the ram's horn used as a trumpet) and possibly from two bulls fighting each other with their horns. So the horn of the wicked or of the righteous symbolizes their strength or victory. Compare Psalms 18:2; 22:21; 89:17; 92:10; 112:9; 148:14.

Cup. A cup of something to drink is often used as an image of the next thing that is going to come your way in life, like the next card you are going to draw. This is what you are being served. Sometimes what is in the cup is good (Pss. 16:5; 23:5; 116:13); sometimes it is bad. Here it is judgment. Compare Psalm 11:6; Isaiah 51:17; Jeremiah 25:15.

REFLECTION: The recurring motif of Psalm 1 distinguishing the righteous and the wicked comes from the mouth of God here: "It is I who judge with equity" (v. 2). The God of Jacob declares, "I will cut off the horns of all the wicked, but the horns of the righteous will be lifted up" (v. 10). Though the earth quakes and all people tremble in fear, wait, for God chooses the appointed time, and he will judge with equity. Perhaps there is no greater test of our trust than waiting for justice, waiting for God's appointment, waiting for his equity, and waiting to be lifted up.

Psalm 76

THEME: The Lord protected his people as a mighty warrior executing justice.

TYPE: Zion song.

AUTHOR: A psalm of Asaph. A song. For the director of music. With stringed instruments.

BACKGROUND: A likely setting for the psalm is a military threat to the southern kingdom of Judah around 735 BC. Several western countries, including Israel and Syria, banded together with the thought of fighting Assyria but then turned on Judah, who wouldn't join them (see Isa. 7–8). Assyria later became a threat to Judah. God protected Judah in both cases, though Assyria came to the very gates of Jerusalem.

STRUCTURE: Four stanzas of three lines each. Verses 1, 4, 7, and 10 develop a theme of praise, declaring God's greatness. Verses 2–3, 5–6, 8–9, and 11–12 develop a related theme of praise, describing God's protective acts and calling on all to fear him. Either theme may be read separately and make sense. The composition weaves them together, suggesting that the two themes may be read or sung by different voices.

SPECIAL NOTES: "Salem," in verse 2, is short for Jerusalem. "His tent" refers to the shelter he provides for his people.

REFLECTION: Our God reigns. The threat of violent attack generates a corresponding desire for justice. God does not manipulate minds to make people choose peace. Those who choose to war against his people meet defeat. God allows people to choose to oppose him, but he overpowers opposition. He acts justly and for justice. Peace comes when his reign is acknowledged.

Psalm 77

© Johan Ramberg/www.istockphoto.com

THEME: Because the people are uncertain of God's current involvement with them, the psalmist leads them in remembering God's past deeds of redemption.

TYPE: Mixed: lament, instruction.

AUTHOR: A psalm (*mizmor*) of Asaph. For the director of music. For Jeduthun.

BACKGROUND: Some distress has come on the nation. It is difficult to know whether the individual speaking is the king or a prophet or priest. Although the speaker is an individual, the psalm concerns the community. Some of the psalm addresses God, as in prayer, while other portions address the people, offering the speaker's thoughts and approach as an example.

STRUCTURE: Stanzas 1 and 2 (vv. 1–2 and 3–6) tell of the psalmist's determination and weariness in crying out to God. Stanza 3 (vv. 7–9) is full of questions, as the psalmist wonders if God has given up on his people.

Stanza 4 (vv. 10–12) should be read as two three-part lines (tricola) that divide the psalm in half. The psalmist first declares the coping strategy of remembering the Lord's former deeds. Then, beginning with 11b, the second half of the psalm addresses God directly, having a form of "you" or "your" in every line. (In the first half, the Hebrew text has only one questionable occurrence of "you" and instead speaks of God to the people.)

Stanza 5 (vv. 13–15) recalls the power and wonder of God's redemption of his people. Stanza 6 (vv. 16–19) specifically revisits his power over the waters. Verse 20 concludes with the specific memory of God leading the people through Moses.

SPECIAL NOTES: The second half of the psalm recalls the exodus. Stanza 5, especially verses 11–13, echoes the Song at the Sea in Exodus 15. The rest of the psalm recalls God's victory over the sea and mentions Moses and Aaron.

REFLECTION: This is a psalm of waiting. The psalmist's soul refuses to be comforted by any means other than the Lord, yet is close enough to despair to wonder if God will ever again be favorable. Instead of staring into a blank space, the psalmist turns to history and recalls God's mighty acts in delivering his people from Egypt. That too was a deliverance that was a long time in coming but magnificent in its redemption. Hope is rooted in the character of God known through his past redemptions. Such hope will persist in bringing lament to God until he hears the groanings of his people and leads them again like a flock.

Psalm 78

THEME: God's faithfulness has outdone Israel's unfaithfulness with rebukes, provision, and leadership.

TYPE: Instruction.

AUTHOR: A *maskil* of Asaph.

BACKGROUND: This psalm gives a sketch of Israel's history from the plagues on Egypt in the early part of Exodus to the reign of David in 1 Samuel. The account highlights Israel's rebellions and God's provision of manna (Ex. 16) and quail (Num. 11). The purpose is to remind Israel not to rebel, a thought that echoes passages such as Deuteronomy 8:11 and 9:7.

STRUCTURE: The many stanzas of the psalm cluster into nine major sections. Verses 1–8 introduce the psalmist's intention to teach the people to trust God and not be rebellious.

Sections 2, 6, and 8 (vv. 9–11, 40–41, and 56–58) indict Israel for its rebellions. They share a number of words in common and also use a large variety of words for turning away and provoking God.

Sections 3 and 4 (vv. 12–20 and 21–30) tell the stories of Israel provoking God in the wilderness, when the people asked for food and God provided first manna and then quail. Section 5 (vv. 31–39) gives commentary on this history, telling how the people often sinned and God was compassionate. Section 7 (vv. 42–44) goes back even farther and recalls the plagues of the exodus and the conquest of the Promised Land. And the last section (vv. 59–72) moves on to the period of the judges leading to the kingship of David. The pattern of Israel's rebellion, God's anger, and then mercy positions David's kingship as part of God's compassionate acts to lead his people well.

SPECIAL NOTES: The term *maskil* in the title may mean either "skillful," which would be a reference to musical performance, or "making prudent," which would invite the reader to contemplation.

© Tom Grill/Corbis

REFLECTION: How often do we consider our responsibility to train and educate our memory? We are responsible not only for what we choose to remember, but for how we remember it. What do we see when we remember? Some see only the glories of their own success in self-flattery as if they were all alone. Others see only the dark places in a long string of disappointments and shame. The way we remember also shapes how we project ourselves into our future; it gives a glimpse of how we will engage our future.

Psalm 79

THEME: The psalmist prays to God for Judah to be delivered and its enemies to be paid back for their evil.

TYPE: Communal lament.

AUTHOR: A psalm (*mizmor*) of Asaph.

BACKGROUND: Jerusalem has suffered a military defeat, and the temple has been defiled. The intense imagery suggests this relates to the fall of Jerusalem to Babylon in 586 BC (2 Kings 25:8–21). Psalm 79:6–7 refers to Jeremiah 10:25 calling for God to pour out his wrath on other nations. This thought is echoed in Psalm 79:12 when asking God to pay back Israel's neighbors. The nearby country of Edom aided Babylon in ransacking Jerusalem. The short book of Obadiah is a prophetic oracle against Edom for its ravaging and plundering. Punishment oracles are leveled against Babylon in Isaiah 13 and 14, Jeremiah 50 and 51, and Habakkuk 2. See also Psalm 137 for imprecations against Babylon. Psalm 79 also connects with Jeremiah 10 in addressing foreign concepts of deity.

STRUCTURE: Psalm 79 has four stanzas of four lines each. Stanza 1 (vv. 1–4) opens with accusations against the invading enemies for looting, killing, and disgracing Judah. Stanza 2 (vv. 5–7) asks how long until the Lord will act, and it petitions him to judge the nations. The central line of the psalm is verse 8a, asking God not to hold the people accountable for their ancestors' sins. Stanza 3 (vv. 8–10b) asks for God's help so that the nations cannot imply that Judah's God has gone missing. Stanza 4 (vv. 10c–13) asks God to pay the enemies back and give his people cause to praise him.

REFLECTION: The psalmist cries out for the judgments of Jeremiah 10:25: "Pour out your wrath on the nations that do not acknowledge you, on the peoples who do not call on your name. For they have devoured Jacob; they have devoured him completely and destroyed his homeland." He calls for the fulfillment of God's wrath against the idolatrous enemies of Israel. This lament actually aids the Israelites in staying true to God, acknowledging their sins, and crying for mercy, yet also resisting the idolatrous influence of those God has used to bring judgment. The prayer ends with a picture of gathered sheep—Israel, the sheep of God's pasture—fulfilling their part in this relationship by praising him.

Psalm 80

THEME: Our only hope in this disaster is that the Lord will look on us favorably and restore us.

TYPE: Communal lament.

AUTHOR: A psalm (*mizmor*) of Asaph. For the director of music. To the tune of "The Lilies of the Covenant."

BACKGROUND: The reference to broken-down walls (v. 12) may suggest the fall of Jerusalem to Babylon in 586 BC (2 Kings 25:8–21).

STRUCTURE: Stanza 1 (vv. 1–3) implores God to listen and save. Stanza 2 (vv. 4–7) complains to God, placing responsibility on him for his people's afflictions. Stanza 3 (vv. 8–13) contrasts their prosperity after God took them from Egypt with their current broken-down state. Stanza 4 (vv. 14–19) petitions God to attend to his people, the vine that he transplanted, and restore them.

Todd Bolen/www.BiblePlaces.com

SPECIAL NOTES: God is called the shepherd of Israel in verse 1. *Shepherd* was a designation for a king in the ancient world.

REFLECTION: As sheep depend on their shepherd, and a vine on the husbandman, the psalmist declares his dependence on God. The dependence is so complete and is felt so keenly that the psalmist seems to boldly risk this accusing language—God has fed his people with the bread of tears, tears by the bowlful, and God has made them an object of derision and mocking. He has broken down the walls of the vineyard; wild animals have ravaged the fruit and torn down the vines, and it is burned with fire. This seems like risky speech. The psalmist stands on the frontier edges of unexplored territory with God, looks honestly at the desolation, and feeling abandoned by God, accuses him. He probably recalls Moses' plea to God not to leave Israel as sheep without a shepherd and recalls the Song of the Vineyard (God's word through Isaiah—5:1–7—regarding the vine). From this perspective, the speech seems less risky. It acknowledges God's predicted judgment on his vine also found in the Song of the Vineyard. But now, because of the relationship to the husbandman, the vine cries out for restoration. The desperate cry is "Hear us, restore us, make your face shine, watch over this vine, revive us, and return to us"—language of abandonment.

This psalm and others like it acknowledge desolation, despair, and abandonment in the lives of the faithful. Together these psalms not only acknowledge, but also embrace and absorb these themes into the ongoing dialogue of redemption, teaching us that there is no place outside of the redemptive reach of God's care.

Psalm 81

© Howard Sandler/www.istockphoto.com

THEME: Remembering God's past deliverance brings a reminder that disobedience diminishes blessings.

TYPE: Instruction (including divine lament).

AUTHOR: Of Asaph. For the director of music. According to *gittith*.

BACKGROUND: This psalm refers to more than the historical event of the exodus. It cites the first of the Ten Commandments (v. 9) and alludes to the covenant God made with Israel. A covenant was a treaty between a king (suzerain) who was lord over other lesser kings (vassals). The covenant had several parts: an introduction ("I am the LORD your God," Ex. 20:2a; Ps. 81:10a), historical background ("who brought you out of the land of Egypt," Ex. 20:2b; Ps. 81:10b), stipulations required of the vassals (Ten Commandments; Ex. 20:3–17; Ps. 81:9), blessings or rewards for obedience (Ex. 23:22–30; Ps. 81:10c), and cursings or punishments for disobedience. Where we might expect to find a counterpart to cursings in the psalm, we instead hear the Lord lament that he cannot bless the people more because of their disobedience.

STRUCTURE: Verses 1–3 call the people to praise God while verses 4–5 give motivation to do so, recalling the historical obligation of praising God for deliverance from slavery. God speaks, beginning in verses 6–7, where he first recalls a range of events from the exodus to the rebellion at Meribah. In verses 8–10 God begins a rebuke that refers back to their covenant relationship. While verses 11–12 indict the people for their failure, verses 13–16 present God's attitude as lamenting that their disobedience thwarts giving them blessings.

SPECIAL NOTES: It is not known whether *gittith* in the title is a musical instrument or a musical style.

Meribah is a place where Israel rebelled, asking, "Is the LORD among us or not?" (see Ex. 17:7 and Num. 20:13). Meribah became a symbol of Israel's rebellion.

REFLECTION: Psalm 81 rehearses the bad attitude of Israel, but it also reveals God's heart. We see his desire to bless his people and his frustration when their sins block his desire. God laments here similarly to parents who get no joy out of punishing but are compelled by their children's bad behavior to correct them. They wish for something greater. They still love. In fact, the correction is evidence of that love (cf. Prov. 13:24; Heb. 12:6; Rev. 3:19). But the Lord longs for something more—that we would have no other gods before him and make a different response of love possible.

Psalm 82

THEME: God condemns those who fail in the duty of seeing justice done and particularly of securing justice for the weak.

TYPE: Instruction.

AUTHOR: A psalm (*mizmor*) of Asaph.

BACKGROUND: The assembly of the "gods" is understood in various ways: a rhetorical reference to false gods and their failings, a reference to angels failing in their responsibilities, a grand way of referring to human rulers who have the responsibility of administering justice. In any case, those expected to dispense justice have not. This accusation of failure is like an element of the lament psalms, which often refer to unjust treatment.

STRUCTURE: The units of the psalm have a symmetrically patterned line structure of 1-3-1-3-1. Verse 1 introduces the scene of God presiding over the divine court. In verses 2–4 God indicts them through a rhetorical question and admonishes them to do justice and defend the weak. The central line (v. 5a) condemns their ignorance. In verses 5–7 God finds them guilty and pronounces punishment. The last verse calls on God to administer justice on the earth.

SPECIAL NOTES: In the Psalms the true God is known to the nations by his mighty acts, protection of his people, blessing on his people, and justice. Compare Psalms 67:4; 72; 76:6–8; 96:9–13; 98:8–9; 99:4; and Deuteronomy 4:6–7.

AP/Wide World Photos

REFLECTION: The psalmists complain of injustice in several laments. Here we see another side of God's desire for justice. God does not simply strike down everyone who sins—otherwise there would be no one left. Further, he has set up hierarchies with different degrees of responsibility allotted to angels and to individuals, and different levels of human government. As God desires that we each act righteously, he desires that those in responsibility care for justice. Will they be perfect every time? Will he strike them down immediately? If he doesn't, does that mean he does not care about justice? May we then be casual about our own righteousness or contribution to defending justice? Psalm 82 is a rebuke against the failure to establish justice. What are we doing to "rescue the weak and needy" and to "deliver them from the hand of the wicked"?

Psalm 83

AP/Wide World Photos

THEME: A call for God to put to shame those who plot against him and his people so that his name will be acknowledged in all the earth.

TYPE: Communal lament.

AUTHOR: A psalm (*mizmor*) of Asaph. A song (*shir*).

BACKGROUND: The countries to the east and north of Israel are listed as plotting against them. The exact occasion is not known, and perhaps the psalm could be used whenever any of these took up arms against Israel or Judah. One possibility is the Syro-Ephraimite war of around 735 BC. Several western countries, including Israel and Syria, banded together with the thought of fighting Assyria but then turned on Judah, who would not join them (see Isa. 7–8).

STRUCTURE: Stanzas 1–3 (vv. 1–8) appeal to God to listen and then have an accusation about the enemies' plans to plot against God's people. The third stanza lists the enemies. Stanzas 4 to 6 (vv. 9–16) ask God to act against them as he has in the past against other enemies and in the manner of a wildfire or tempestuous storm. Stanza 6 reveals the desired outcome that people turn to God. Stanza 7 (vv. 17–18) closes with the wish that when the evil plotters are put to shame, the Lord's name will be exalted.

SPECIAL NOTES: God defeated Sisera and Jabin through Deborah, Barak, and Jael in Judges 4. God defeated Oreb and Zeeb of Midian through Gideon in Judges 7:25–8:3. These battles occur in northern and eastern portions of Israel, making them particularly relevant in view of the location of the countries listed in this psalm.

REFLECTION: Little has changed. The descendants of Ishmael, Esau, and Lot—Israel's neighbors—still plot Israel's destruction. In the language of Psalm 1, the psalmist prays that God will make them "like chaff before the wind." Interestingly, this judgment has a stated purpose: "that they will seek your name" and "know that you alone are the Most High over all the earth" (vv. 16, 18). Perhaps this refers to onlookers seeing the destruction of Israel's enemies, but would that not also include the enemies themselves? The cry for justice, however impassioned and bitter, is also governed here by a longing for God's glory to be known even by those being judged—he alone is the Lord of the earth.

Psalm 84

THEME: The highest value one can hold is the desire to dwell with God at his house.

TYPE: Zion song; pilgrimage song.

AUTHOR: A psalm (*mizmor*) of the Sons of Korah. For the director of music. According to *gittith*.

BACKGROUND: Several of the Jewish festivals included a trip to Jerusalem. See, for example, Deuteronomy 14:24 and 16:2, 6, 11.

STRUCTURE: Stanzas 1 and 3 each have seven lines and end with a wisdom saying about the person who is "blessed." The center stanza also begins with a saying about who is "blessed." Stanza 1 (vv. 1–5) speaks with longing of being at God's dwelling, his temple in Jerusalem. Stanza 2 (vv. 6–8) reflects the pilgrimage journey to Jerusalem. Stanza 3 (vv. 9–12) begins with a prayer for the king (the anointed). Then it continues with praise that in part serves as admonition about the values of putting God first (v. 10) and keeping one's behavior blameless (v. 11).

SPECIAL NOTES: The Lord's name occurs seven times, and "God" (Elohim) occurs seven times. "LORD Almighty" occurs in the first and last lines.

It is not known whether *gittith* in the title is a musical instrument or a musical style.

A blameless life (v. 11) is also referred to in Psalms 15:2; 26:1, 11; 101:2, 6; and 119:1.

Todd Bolen/www.BiblePlaces.com

© Feng Yu/www.istockphoto.com

REFLECTION: Where do you most like to go, and what do you most like to do? Enjoying various places and things is certainly fine, but do we value coming into the Lord's presence in worship with his people more? Do we really think it is better to spend a day in his courts than at the mall, at the game, at the movies, or before the television? Is worship something central that we plan our lives around or something that we fit into a busy schedule?

Psalm 85

THEME: The Lord intends peace for his afflicted yet repentant people but warns them to stay away from folly.

TYPE: Communal lament.

AUTHOR: A psalm (*mizmor*) of the Sons of Korah. For the director of music.

STRUCTURE: The psalm has four stanzas and divides into two halves of seven lines each. Stanza 1 (vv. 1–3) praises God for his past favor and forgiveness for his people. Stanza 2 (vv. 4–7) asks God to restore his favor and asks how long he will be angry. In stanza 3 (vv. 8–9) the psalmist relays God's good intentions for his people, though warning them not to return to folly. The community responds to this prophetic declaration with praise in stanza 4 (vv. 10–13).

SPECIAL NOTES: Praise is often present in communal laments, an affirmation that God is the right one to turn to even though the present circumstances are difficult.

REFLECTION: "What have you done for me lately?" That question dismisses the past as if only current circumstances count, as if they are the only measure of a relationship. It is the manipulative question of the fickle. This psalm models the opposite. The yearning of the present is informed by the past. God has forgiven and turned from anger in the past. This informs our present so that we will not place our fickle and demanding attitude on God. In faithfulness we voice our complaint and anticipate that righteousness and peace will meet and embrace.

Psalm 86

THEME: The psalmist turns to the Lord in the midst of distress because only the Lord really answers, and he is rich in loyal love.

TYPE: Individual lament.

AUTHOR: A prayer of David.

BACKGROUND: In Exodus 34 God replaced the tablets of the Ten Commandments after Moses broke the first tablets in anger over Israel's sin. In Exodus 34:6 God revealed himself to Moses, declaring first those qualities mentioned in Psalm 86:15. This became the foundational theology of God's forgiving and loyal character. Here the psalmist depends on God's nature being so in order to pray with confidence.

STRUCTURE: Psalm 86 has three major sections. The stanzas from verses 1–7 implore God to listen and act on the psalmist's behalf. The reasons on the one hand are that the psalmist is needy, troubled, and trusts God and, on the other hand, that the Lord is forgiving, good, loving, and one who answers. To actually be a God who answers makes the Lord unique, as verses 8–10 affirm that the nations have no such God and will all come to worship the Lord because of his great deeds. Verses 11–17 petition God to train the psalmist in obedience and to protect from enemies.

SPECIAL NOTES: Exodus 34:6, the basis for Psalm 86:15, is also reflected in Nehemiah 9:17; Psalms 103:8; 145:8; Joel 2:13; and Jonah 4:2.

REFLECTION: Here the psalmist declares what makes the God of Israel unique—he is compassionate and gracious, slow to anger, abounding in love and faithfulness. This recurring theme distinguishes the God of Israel and sets him apart above all others; he is desired above all. How does the psalmist approach this one-of-a-kind God in this lament? "Teach me your way, Lord, that I may rely on your faithfulness; give me an undivided heart, that I may fear your name" (v. 11). This is his pledge of allegiance, his request for a loyal heart. In this, he instructs us to recognize God's uniqueness, that he alone is God and the only abiding source of compassion and merciful loving-kindness. He models for us loyalty to this God who saves because of his loving faithfulness. In this spirit the psalmist cries out for deliverance, for a sign of God's goodness. And he pledges to praise God with all his heart and glorify his name forever.

Psalm 87

THEME: The Lord designates Zion as his favorite place; it is a privilege to be born there.

TYPE: Zion song.

AUTHOR: A psalm (*mizmor*) of the Sons of Korah. A song (*shir*).

BACKGROUND: God told Moses in advance that once the people were in the land, he would choose a place for his name to dwell (Deut. 12:3, 5, 11, 21) and where the people should worship. He solidified this with King David and verified it with Solomon (1 Kings 8:29).

STRUCTURE: The affirmation "This one was born in Zion," in verse 4 stands at the exact center of the psalm. Stanza 1 (vv. 1–4) declares the Lord's love for Zion and boasts of the one born there. Stanza 2 (vv. 5–7) restates his boast.

SPECIAL NOTES: The reference to other nations has been understood in various ways, but what is clear is that it is a special privilege to be associated with Zion. "Rahab" may refer to Egypt (not the woman of Josh. 2).

Todd Bolen/www.BiblePlaces.com

REFLECTION: When God made his covenant with David, which included that David's son would build the temple, God included bold words like "forever." Because God is omnipotent and eternal, his choice of Israel has given specific shape to Israelite and even world history. And what a privilege it will be to be a citizen of the New Jerusalem (Rev. 21:2)!

Psalm 88

THEME: The psalmist asks to be spared from the grave and expresses feeling rejected and overwhelmed by God's wrath.

TYPE: Individual lament.

AUTHOR: A psalm (*mizmor*) of the Sons of Korah. A song (*shir*). For the director of music. According to *mahalath leannoth*. A *maskil* of Heman the Ezrahite.

BACKGROUND: While the background is not certain, it seems to envision the despair of a wounded soldier or someone with a life-threatening illness.

STRUCTURE: Stanzas 1 and 2 (vv. 1–2 and 3–5) appeal to God to listen and lament the psalmist's distress, being near to death. Stanzas 3 and 4 (vv. 6–9a and 9b–12) complain of how harsh God has been. Nevertheless, the psalmist turns to God daily and as a motive for restoration asks rhetorically whether the dead give God any praise. Stanzas 5 and 6 (vv. 13–14 and 15–17) give evidence that the psalmist has some measure of confidence in God—that is, he prays daily, even while wondering if God has rejected him. Finally, the psalmist laments over personal distress and complains of God's wrath (v. 18).

SPECIAL NOTES: The meaning of *mahalath* in the title is uncertain but may relate to entreating. It occurs only here and in Psalm 53. *Leannoth* may come from a root meaning "for singing" or a root meaning "for afflictions."

The term *maskil* in the title may mean either "skillful," which would be a reference to musical performance, or "making prudent," which would invite the reader to contemplation.

REFLECTION: "I have borne your terrors and am in despair ... your terrors have destroyed me." The darkest of the laments, this psalm bears witness to extreme human experience. If Psalm 22 is a psalm for Good Friday, this is a psalm for Holy Saturday—not surprisingly one of the least observed holy days in the Christian year. The psalm ends not in praise, nor any statement of confidence, but in darkness, despair, and abandonment. Some have written that this psalm could never be on the lips of a Christian—it seems too hopeless, too depressing. But only poetry of witness like this seems to catch and hold extreme experiences like death and burial; it seems a fitting coda to "My God, my God, why have you forsaken me?" (Mk. 15:34; Mt. 27:46). Words cannot describe the personal holocausts of some individuals and communities. "Waves" and "flood," "pits," "darkness," and "despair"—only these begin to touch the experiences of some who have chosen to become disciples of a slaughtered Lamb. This poetry, far from denying Christ's victory over death, invites us into the very heart of it, the very thing that sets his message apart—he defeats death by entering it.

Psalm 89

THEME: The people celebrate God's covenant with David and his sons but then lament their current distress.

TYPE: Royal.

AUTHOR: A *maskil* of Ethan the Ezrahite.

Ryan McVay

BACKGROUND: God made a covenant with David in 2 Samuel 7, promising him an enduring dynasty and a special relationship with the son who would follow him on the throne. Second Samuel 7:14 says that God will be like a father to him and he like a son to God. This thought is also expressed in the center stanza of the middle section of the psalm (vv. 26–29).

STRUCTURE: In the first four lines (vv. 1–4), first the king speaks of proclaiming God's loyalty, and then God speaks affirming the Davidic covenant. The next fourteen lines (vv. 5–18) praise him as God of gods and ruler of heaven and earth. The people who know him are blessed, and their shield, the king, belongs to the Lord. In the next twenty lines (vv. 19–37), we hear the Lord's voice recounting his promises of the Davidic covenant and the requirements of the Davidic heirs. The next fourteen lines (vv. 38–51) contrast these promises with the people's complaint that God has rejected his anointed and allowed enemies to be victorious and ask how long this will be so. Verse 52 closes the psalm and book 3 of the Psalter with a line of praise to the Lord.

SPECIAL NOTES: The term *maskil* in the title may mean either "skillful," which would be a reference to musical performance, or "making prudent," which would invite the reader to contemplation.

Horn. This imagery of the horn comes from bulls (not the ram's horn used as a trumpet) and possibly from two bulls fighting each other with their horns. So the horn of the wicked or of the righteous symbolizes their strength or victory. Compare Psalms 18:2; 22:21; 75:4–5, 10; 92:10; 112:9; 148:14.

REFLECTION: The king's special place in the community comes to the forefront in this psalm as the fortunes of the covenant community and the heir of the Davidic covenant are intertwined. The community's complaint is rooted in the past-known faithfulness of God. On this basis they express their disorientation at defeat and a disgraced king. And on this basis they remain oriented toward God. In disappointment they are holding on to his promises.

Psalm **90**

THEME: Like withering grass before an eternal God, the people ask for perspective, mercy, and blessing.

TYPE: Communal lament.

AUTHOR: A prayer of Moses the man of God.

BACKGROUND: The title's attribution to Moses and the concern over people dying calls to mind the wilderness wanderings: "The LORD's anger burned against Israel and he made them wander in the wilderness forty years, until the whole generation of those who had done evil in his sight was gone" (Num. 32:13). The specific background is actually uncertain, but the psalm was certainly fit for large-scale national punishment or disasters that took many lives.

STRUCTURE: Stanza 1 (vv. 1–2) opens by praising God as creator and sustainer throughout generations. Stanza 2 (vv. 3–6) seems half praise and half complaint. It acknowledges God's power over life and death, realized as sweeping people away like grass. Stanza 3 (vv. 7–12) expresses dismay at the reality of death and terror at God's anger. This leads to the request to be taught a proper perspective on the brevity of human life. Stanzas 4 and 5 (vv. 13–16 and v. 17) petition God to return and bring joy to match the past affliction. They also look ahead to the future of the nation.

SPECIAL NOTES: Psalm 90 begins book 4 of the Psalter.

Second Peter 3:8 refers to Psalm 90:4.

REFLECTION: We easily see how a generation of Israelites dying off in the wilderness over forty years would feel a sense of futility. Funerals may have been a daily experience and constant expectation. They must have wondered *How long until something different, something better?* All humanity is under the sentence of death and feels the affliction of the curse. We yearn to be free of both but feel their weight, though with different amounts of oppression from time to time. A forward-looking hope directs the petitions for something better. Such satisfaction is all the more realized as good news when the sense of futility has been fully embraced. Hope is brighter when hopelessness is known. The short-lived psalmist roots this hope in the eternal God.

Psalm 91

THEME: God will protect the one who trusts in him.

TYPE: Mixed: confidence, instruction, possibly royal.

AUTHOR: Unknown.

BACKGROUND: The priestly blessing and prophetic oracle, likely given at the temple, suggest a liturgy. The terminology of traveling and possibly war suggests that the psalm may have been used in a ceremony when facing a military threat, and so verse 2 may express the voice of the king. On the other hand, while the dangers of going to war are not limited to the actual battles, the presence of dangers unrelated to battle may indicate that the psalm was used for traveling worshipers. In this context, attacks are not from soldiers but from the wicked generally or demonic powers.

© John Cancalosi/www.naturepl.com

STRUCTURE: The psalm begins with a brief interchange between two speakers, probably the king and a prophet or priest. We then hear prophetic instruction followed by God speaking in a prophetic oracle.

In stanza 1 (vv. 1–2), a prophetic or priestly voice announces the one who relies on the Most High; then this person, possibly the king or a traveling worshiper, affirms his trust in God. In stanzas 2 and 3 (vv. 3–8 and 9–13) the prophet/priest proclaims God's protection. Stanza 4 (vv. 14–16) presents a prophetic oracle in which God assures that he will answer the prophet/priest with protection and long life.

SPECIAL NOTES: The idea of God's protection on the dwelling of the righteous also appears in Proverbs 3:33 and Job 5:24. The concept of God's protection as it appears in Proverbs 3:21–26 has similarities to Psalm 91.

An ironic case of seeing God's payback with the eyes only (cf. v. 8) occurs in 2 Kings 6:24–7:20. Second Kings 19 records a case of thousands falling without God's people fighting.

In Matthew 4:6 and Luke 4:10–11, Satan applies Psalm 91:11–12 to Jesus, tempting him to jump off the pinnacle of the temple as proof that he is the Messiah. Jesus extends the application of Psalm 91:13 to the seventy he sent on a mission to proclaim the Good News in Luke 10:19.

REFLECTION: Jesus' response to Satan in the gospel accounts confirms that the psalm of confidence is an expression of placing hope in God, not a guarantee that sets aside caution or presumes invincibility. Promises of protection and power should not lead to arrogant folly. Satan wanted to incite Jesus to abuse the promise by demanding a miracle from God, but Jesus countered with Deuteronomy 6:16, declaring it wrong to put God to the test. When Jesus granted the disciples power over demonic powers, he told them not to rejoice because those powers were subject to them, but to rejoice instead because their names were recorded in heaven.

Psalm 92

THEME: The Lord is exalted; he will defeat his enemies and empower the righteous.

TYPE: Hymn of thanksgiving.

AUTHOR: Unknown. A psalm (*mizmor*). A song (*shir*). For the Sabbath day.

STRUCTURE: Psalm 92 has a single line (v. 8) at its center. Stanza 1 (vv. 1–4) revels in how good it is to praise God with music. Stanza 2 (vv. 5–7) praises God for his great deeds and ideas. In contrast, the wicked and the fool do not even understand their own temporary nature. Verse 8 declares the Lord exalted. Stanza 3 (vv. 9–11) states confidently that the Lord's enemies will perish and that the psalmist, probably the king, will be given victory over his enemies. Stanza 4 (vv. 12–15) extends that confidence, or perhaps a blessing, to the people who are righteous.

SPECIAL NOTES: *Horn*. This imagery of the horn comes from bulls (not the ram's horn used as a trumpet) and possibly from two bulls fighting each other with their horns. So the horn of the wicked or of the righteous symbolizes their strength or victory. Compare Psalms 18:2; 22:21; 75:4–5, 10; 89:17; 112:9; 148:14.

REFLECTION: Reminiscent of Psalm 1, Psalm 92 contrasts the flourishing of the righteous and the downfall of the wicked. But it adds a perspective on the viewpoint of the wicked. They are so caught up in delusion, they cannot see their plight or end. They are like those who drink themselves to drunkenness to be the life of the party, then make fools of themselves and later cause a car wreck. They are like those who prize the acceptance of their friends so highly that they engage in dangerous or illegal behavior. In the end they come to ruin and cannot say of the Lord, "He is my Rock" (v. 15).

Psalm 93

THEME: The Lord reigns and has firmly established his throne, the earth, and his law.

TYPE: Hymn of praise (celebration of the Lord's kingship).

AUTHOR: Unknown.

BACKGROUND: The myths of the surrounding nations sometimes pit their gods against a watery chaos or against a god associated with the seas and with death or chaos. Such imagery may have been inspired by fierce storms over or coming from the Mediterranean. Psalm 93 takes this concern and names Israel's God, the Lord, as the one who is more powerful than the violent waters. He has established his throne, the earth, and his law. The imagery led the translator of the Septuagint, an ancient Greek translation, to link the psalm to the day before the Sabbath as the time when the earth was established. (The Septuagint also labeled the psalm as "a praise song of David.")

STRUCTURE: Stanza 1 (vv. 1–2) praises the Lord for his strength and for establishing both his throne and the earth. Stanza 2 (vv. 3–4) affirms the power of the sea but declares the Lord to be more powerful. The last stanza (v. 5) celebrates the Lord's enduring reign.

SPECIAL NOTES: The Lord's house (v. 5) refers to his heavenly temple.

REFLECTION: "Mightier than the breakers of the sea—the Lord on high is mighty" (v. 4). The oceans are powerful forces regulating global temperature and the weather. They are home to incredible numbers of living things of wildly different shapes and sizes. Sailors throughout history describe a deep and abiding reverence and awe of the oceans' tremendous power. But in Mark 4, when a furious squall arises on a sea so that waves are breaking over the disciples' boat, Jesus rebukes the wind and the waves, saying, " 'Quiet! Be still!' Then the wind died down and it was completely calm." Mighty indeed.

Psalm 94

THEME: The king calls on God to enact justice and affirms his reliance on the Lord.

TYPE: Mixed: communal lament, royal.

AUTHOR: Unknown.

BACKGROUND: Clearly Psalm 94 contains concerns related to the whole community. Verses 4 and 14 refer to the people as a whole and verse 5 to members of the community. But they do not speak as a group. The individual who does speak is likely the king, whose fate as an individual is most closely associated with that of the nation.

STRUCTURE: Most of the stanzas have four lines, with the exception of the first stanza, which has three lines. The odd number of total lines places the blessing formula in verse 12 at the center of the psalm.

Stanza 1 (vv. 1–3) calls on God to justly pay back the proud. Stanza 2 (vv. 4–7) accuses the wicked not only of arrogantly oppressing the weak but claiming that God does not notice or care. Stanza 3 (vv. 8–11) speaks with a prophetic voice admonishing the enemies as fools who underestimate God. Stanza 4 (vv. 12–15) pronounces blessing on those who accept God's discipline and confidently asserts that the Lord will come through with justice for his people. Stanza 5 (vv. 16–19) gives a testimony of the Lord's protection. In stanza 6 (vv. 20–23) the psalmist demonstrates trust in God and separation from the wicked.

SPECIAL NOTES: The gender-specific reference in verse 12 to the "man" (NIV), whom the Lord instructs from his Law, probably refers to the king. Deuteronomy 17:18–20 instructs the king to make his own copy of the Law. He is to read it every day to learn to fear and obey God and so that his descendants will prosper.

REFLECTION: A loving and compassionate king intercedes for his people; he laments, "How long will the wicked be jubilant?" (v. 3). The wicked are killing the strangers, the widows, and the orphans; they are crushing and oppressive. The king allows us to see his great vulnerabilities—he is overwhelmed and feels helpless; his anxiety is great. He attributes an unfailing love to God, whose consolation brings joy. And in the process he reveals that God has become his fortress, the rock in whom he takes refuge. These prayers of lament become the cords that bind the king to God, his fortress—the means by which he takes refuge—and they are examples for us, binding us to him as well.

Psalm 95

© Oleg Prikhodko/www.istockphoto.com

THEME: The Lord is King; do not rebel as Israel did in the wilderness.

TYPE: Mixed: hymn of praise (celebration of the Lord's kingship), instruction.

AUTHOR: Unknown.

BACKGROUND: After God brought Israel out of Egypt and to the border of the Promised Land, the people feared to enter the land and rebelled. God condemned them to wander in the wilderness for forty years (v. 10) while those over twenty years old died off (Num. 14:21–23, 28–35; 32:10–13). This psalm contrasts God's kingship with the people's rebellion and expresses God's yearning for the people to obey.

STRUCTURE: A praise hymn with three stanzas is followed by a unit of instruction. The first stanza (vv. 1–2) is a call to praise. Stanza 2 (vv. 3–5) praises God as king and creator. Stanza 3 (vv. 6–7) is a call to praise followed by motivation to praise God. The fourth stanza (vv. 8–11) represents a shift. The prophetic voice expresses the frustrated desire that God's people would obey. Thereafter we hear several quotes from the Lord warning them not to repeat their former disobedience.

SPECIAL NOTES: Psalm 95:7 and 11 are alluded to in Hebrews 3:7, 15, 18.

Meribah is a place where Israel rebelled, asking, "Is the LORD among us or not?" See Exodus 17:7 and Numbers 20:13. Meribah became a symbol of Israel's rebellion. For Massah, see also Deuteronomy 6:16. For their pattern of complaining despite God's grace and provision, see Numbers 11:1, 4; 12:1; 14:1–2; 16:1, 41; 20:2–3.

REFLECTION: Presumption is a danger of receiving grace (cf. Rom. 6:1). After the Lord delivered the Israelites from Egypt and made his covenant with them at Sinai and it was time to move on to the Promised Land, the people became complainers. A time of ease led to an unwillingness to make an effort and endure some hardship. Privilege led to demandingness. This psalm counters this tendency by pairing the exaltation of praise for provision with the warning not to repeat the presumptions of the past. Do praise the Lord for his mighty acts of salvation. But do not expect ease and only ease. Kneel before him and submit.

Psalm 96

THEME: The Lord is most worthy of praise; proclaim his kingship to the nations.

TYPE: Hymn of praise (celebration of the Lord's kingship).

AUTHOR: Unknown.

BACKGROUND: First Chronicles 16 utilizes Psalm 96 when recounting bringing the ark of the covenant to Jerusalem. It records how David brought the ark to Jerusalem and gave Asaph and his relatives responsibility for praising the Lord. First Chronicles 16:8–22 corresponds to Psalm 105:1–15 and commemorates God's covenant with Abraham and protection of the patriarchs. Psalm 105 continues on to commemorate God delivering Israel from Egypt, whereas 1 Chronicles 16:23–33 instead incorporates Psalm 96, though with slight differences.

STRUCTURE: Stanza 1 (vv. 1–3) is a call to praise the Lord, making him known among the nations. Stanza 2 (vv. 4–6) provides the motivation for praise, which is that the Lord is a great God, the heaven-maker, not just an idol. The central lines of the poem, stanza 3 (vv. 7–9), call the whole world to worship him as is his due. Stanza 4 (vv. 10–13) matches stanzas 1 and 2 in length and structure. It proclaims to the nations that the Lord reigns and calls the world to rejoice, for he brings justice.

SPECIAL NOTES: Psalms 96–98 share certain themes with Isaiah 40–55, such as the universal rule of the Lord.

In the Psalms, the Lord being made known as God to the nations is often connected to his mighty deeds, his salvation for Israel, and his justice.

Todd Bolen/www.BiblePlaces.com

Digital Stock

Digital Vision

REFLECTION: Identity theft. Someone perhaps gets ahold of your social security number or your bank account numbers, but certainly your name. They claim to be you. Your reputation is marred, and others are not sure who you are (or who is you) and what you have done. God is a victim of identity theft. In the ancient world there were many "worthless idols" posing as deity. In the modern world, many false philosophies and value systems compete for God's proper place. This psalm tries to set the record straight. It boldly declares the Lord's reign and calls for all to give him the glory due his name. It is great cause for joy—our God reigns.

Psalm 97

© Striking-Photography/www.BigStockPhoto.com

THEME: The Lord reigns over all the earth; his power shames idol worshipers and brings joy to the righteous.

TYPE: Hymn of praise (celebration of the Lord's kingship).

AUTHOR: Unknown.

STRUCTURE: Psalm 97 has two main sections divided by verse 7 as the central line. Verses 1–6 proclaim that the Lord reigns and describe his power like a lightning storm, so that all see his glory. Verse 7 declares the futility of worshiping idols. Verses 8–12 record the joy of God's people and call them to righteousness.

SPECIAL NOTES: Verse 7 calls on the "gods" to worship the Lord. On the one hand, there aren't really any other gods, but the metaphor asserts the superiority of the Lord. On the other hand, there are other spiritual beings. The Greek translation of the Psalms, called the Septuagint, translated "gods" as spiritual beings, that is angels. Hebrews 1:6 then applies Psalm 97:7 to Jesus, as superior to the angels.

Psalms 96–98 share certain themes with Isaiah 40–55, such as the universal rule of the Lord.

In the Psalms the Lord being made known as God to the nations is often connected to his mighty deeds, his salvation for Israel, and his justice.

REFLECTION: The Lord reigns. This thesis has far-reaching implications. The glory and righteousness of the Lord that are proclaimed by the heavens put to shame those who worship mere statues (vv. 6–7). The Lord is known through his mighty acts in creation (vv. 3–5), his just rule (vv. 2, 8), and the deliverance of his people (vv. 10–11; cf. Ps. 67). And the Lord is not like other "gods," who rule a certain portion of land or a country, but is over all the earth (v. 9). There are certain basic tenets of faith that should define everything about our lives, such as monotheism (there is only one God), the Trinity, humanity as God's image, humanity as fallen—sinful and cursed—redemption through repentance and substitutionary atonement, the responsibility of parents to train their children, and so on. But first on the list is this: the Lord reigns.

Psalm 98

THEME: Praise the Lord with energy and music for his faithful salvation and justice for the earth.

TYPE: Hymn of praise (celebration of the Lord's kingship).

AUTHOR: Unknown. A psalm (*mizmor*).

BACKGROUND: This psalm celebrates the Lord's victories. The Lord's strong arm, hand, or right hand are used frequently when describing his mighty acts. The psalm need not stand in the background of any one act in particular but could be used for the celebration of any.

STRUCTURE: Stanza 1 (vv. 1–3) begins with a call to praise but mainly praises the Lord for his salvation on behalf of Israel, seen to the ends of the earth. Stanza 2 (vv. 4–6) is entirely a call to praise, to sing and shout with instruments before the Lord. Stanza 3 (vv. 7–9) continues the call to praise, extending it to parts of creation. The basis in this section is that the Lord judges the world and does so with equity.

SPECIAL NOTES: Psalms 96–98 share certain themes with Isaiah 40–55, such as the universal rule of the Lord.

In the Psalms the Lord being made known as God to the nations is often connected to his mighty deeds, his salvation for Israel, and his justice.

Luca Della Robbia (1400–1482)/Museo dell'Opera del Duomo, Florence, Italy/The Bridgeman Art Library

REFLECTION: It is interesting to note the language referring to salvation in this psalm. Here it is not our salvation (as we usually refer to it) but God's salvation, "All the ends of the earth have seen the salvation of our God" (v. 3). This is a powerful vision, heaven calling the whole earth to ecstatic praise—"Shout for joy to the LORD, all the earth, burst into jubilant song" (v. 4)—because God has worked his salvation with his strong and holy arm. Perhaps the apostle Paul had this vision in mind—mountains singing, rivers clapping their hands, and the sea resounding—when he wrote, "The creation itself will be liberated from its bondage to decay and brought into the freedom and glory of the children of God" (Rom. 8:21). How much more ecstatic should our praise be as we enter our freedom and glory after we have groaned inwardly as in the pains of childbirth while waiting eagerly for our redemption.

Psalm 99

THEME: The Lord reigns over all with justice and has proven himself to his faithful servants in the past.

TYPE: Hymn of praise (celebration of the Lord's kingship), Zion song.

AUTHOR: Unknown.

BACKGROUND: This psalm is normally classified as a hymn of praise or an "enthronement" psalm. It also specifically praises God as great in Zion, though it does not mention Jerusalem as extensively as the psalms traditionally called Zion songs.

STRUCTURE: This psalm has four stanzas of three lines each. Stanzas 1, 2, and 4 end by declaring the Lord to be holy. The beginning of verse 5 and verse 9 are identical, closing the two halves of the psalm.

Stanza 1 (vv. 1–3) mixes statements of praise with calls to praise. The big idea is that the Lord reigns over all peoples, who in turn should praise him. Stanza 2 (vv. 4–5) proclaims the Lord's justice for Israel and then makes another call to worship. Stanza 3 (vv. 6–7) is instructive in that it reviews how God answered his faithful servants in the past. Stanza 4 (vv. 8–9) praises God for answering them and makes another call to worship the Lord.

SPECIAL NOTES: In the Psalms the Lord being made known as God to the nations is often connected to his mighty deeds, his salvation for Israel, and his justice.

That he sits "enthroned between the cherubim" refers to the Lord's presence above the ark of the covenant. The ark of the covenant is described in Exodus 25. Two golden cherubim (representations of angels) were atop the "mercy seat" forming a lid for the ark. God's presence ("shekinah glory") came to the tabernacle and later to the temple to rest above the ark.

Gerth Medien

REFLECTION: Psalm 99 exalts in the Lord's reign over all the earth and calls on the leaders of the people to carefully consider their role under the heading of the Lord's reign. By bringing up prominent leaders of the past, such as Moses and Samuel, the psalm invites current leaders to consider how they keep company with them. These men called on the Lord, kept his statutes, and found forgiveness in God. But the story is equally if not more so about God—he answered them, he forgave them, and he held them accountable. Lead like they did. But remember, leaders, you do not rule. He does.

Psalm 100

THEME: The singers call people to worship and declare God's faithfulness to them with gratitude.

TYPE: Hymn of praise.

AUTHOR: Unknown. A psalm (*mizmor*). For giving grateful praise.

BACKGROUND: The title suggests that the psalm was used when making a thanksgiving offering (a type of peace offering described in Lev. 3). The regulations for thanksgiving offerings appear in Leviticus 7:11 15; 22:29–30. The worshipers would make an animal sacrifice with unleavened bread and also share the food in a communal meal. They would sing this psalm perhaps as part of entering the courtyards around the temple or as a prelude to a time of declaring what the Lord has done for them.

STRUCTURE: This short psalm has four three-part lines (tricola). The first and third (vv. 1–2 and 4) are calls to praise. The second line (v. 3) promotes a humble attitude by reminding that God is our maker. The last line (v. 5) furnishes a reason for praise—that the Lord's faithful love endures across the generations.

SPECIAL NOTES: The perspective is global (all the earth, v. 1), but the location is particular (his courts, v. 4).

REFLECTION: The people whose stories fill them with thanks to God shout these lines with joy and invite others to come and hear about God's protection and provision in their lives. These others are invited in, even if their own stories are not full of thanks at the moment. For the call to praise is primarily motivated by God's works and character and not dependent on our mood. This is not to say that our emotional framework has no bearing on our worship (cf. the story of Hannah in 1 Sam. 1). The many kinds of psalms show that they are fitted to different kinds of circumstances. But consider also Nehemiah's words, "The joy of the Lord is your strength" (Neh. 8:10). The people mourned when they heard the words of the Lord read by Ezra. But Nehemiah and the Levites told them to celebrate because it was a holy day to the Lord. The Lord is our source of joy, and we should take strength from that.

This psalm calls us to praise. "We are his people, the sheep of his pasture" (v. 3); "his love endures forever" (v. 5). These are precious thoughts. Let us enter his gates with thanksgiving.

Psalm 101

THEME: The king purposes to do justice: to oppose and overcome the wicked and honor the faithful.

TYPE: Royal.

AUTHOR: Of David.

BACKGROUND: In this ceremony celebrating the king's rule, the king declares his commitment to ruling justly. A just rule is seen as a threat to the wicked. We infer that this is a royal psalm from the reference to silencing all the wicked in the land. The scope is too broad for the common person, but the king's model of disassociating from the wicked and choosing and rewarding the righteous should be followed by all.

STRUCTURE: The psalm divides into seven stanzas of two two-part lines (bicola). Six of these are easily associated in pairs. In stanzas 1 and 2 (vv. 1–2a and 2b–3a) the king states his intent to praise the Lord for his love and justice and to live a blameless life. Stanzas 3 and 4 (vv. 3b–4 and 5) state his intense opposition to the wicked: the perverse, the haughty, slanderers. In stanza 5 (v. 6) the Lord promises favor for the faithful who lead a blameless life. In stanzas 6 and 7 (vv. 7 and 8) he rejects the deceitful and promises to destroy the wicked.

SPECIAL NOTES: A blameless life (vv. 2, 6) is also referred to in Psalms 15:2; 26:1; 11:84; and 119:1.

REFLECTION: This is a king's pledge, a bold declaration of commitment to live a disciplined life—guarding his eyes, his heart, his mind, and his house; blessing the faithful; silencing slanderers; and so on. What is interesting is that it is not a quid pro quo like other pledges—if you do this, I'll do that. In fact, there's no guarantee that God will even be present (v. 2: "When will you come to me?"). This leader's pledge stands out even more because it is an unconditional declaration without evidence of reciprocity or reply. What will we declare, what will we pledge in commitment simply because our God is loving and just?

Psalm 102

THEME: The psalmist asks that, instead of his life being shortened, it may be written that God heard and answered him so that future generations will praise God.

TYPE: Individual lament, possibly royal.

AUTHOR: Unknown. A prayer of an afflicted person who has grown weak and pours out his lament before the LORD.

BACKGROUND: Because the main speaker is an individual, the psalm is usually taken as an individual lament. But the psalm is clearly concerned with the community when it mentions a future generation, Zion, and the nations. As such, the speaker may well be the king, another national leader, or even a personification of Jerusalem (which would make it a communal lament). In any case, the title of the psalm suggests that any common person may take hold of the psalm as his or her own.

STRUCTURE: In stanza 1 (vv. 1–5) the psalmist makes an initial appeal to be heard and begins to lament the current distress. Stanza 2 (vv. 6–11) continues the lament, illustrating loneliness and complaining about enemy scorn. Stanza 3 (vv. 12–17) is a statement of confidence that God will pity Zion. Stanza 4 (vv. 18–22) petitions God to act by asking that future generations be able to look back and say that God indeed saw and heard from heaven. Stanza 5 (vv. 23–28) returns to lament, contrasting how the psalmist's days seem to be shortened but God is eternal.

SPECIAL NOTES: Withering grass pictures the short life of humanity in general, or of the wicked, in several passages: Psalms 37:2; 102:4, 11; 129:6; Isaiah 15:6; 40:7–8; James 1:11; 1 Peter 1:24.

REFLECTION: The precariousness of the psalmist's life leads in four directions. (1) Lament over personal distress. The psalmist does not "stuff" his feelings inside. But neither does he simply "dump" the feelings out as if unloading is the only goal. He fully expresses them with intent and direction as part of turning to God. (2) Recognition of God's eternal and reliable nature. It is the content of praise and the foundation for hope. (3) Realization that God's plan, like himself, stretches across generations. (4) The petition to be included in the transgenerational story of God's rescue of prisoners as the praise of the eternal one continues in the community of his children, continuing from generation to generation.

Psalm 103

THEME: Praise the Lord for his just rule and enduring love.

TYPE: Hymn of praise.

AUTHOR: Of David.

BACKGROUND: The speakers in the psalm include both an individual and a group. Its praise content indicates that it may have been used in a setting such as that of a thanksgiving sacrifice, which also included sharing a meal with others. The thanksgiving offering (a type of peace offering) is described in Leviticus 3 and 7:11–15; 22:29–30.

STRUCTURE: Psalm 103 is partially symmetrical. The middle of the psalm has two stanzas of six lines, bounded on either side by a single line. The psalm's beginning and end both carry instructions to bless the Lord, though they do not have the same number of lines.

Stanza 1 (vv. 1–5) is a call to praise that lists several reasons to do so. Verse 6 is a single line of praise declaring the Lord's justice. Stanzas 2 and 3 (vv. 7–12 and 13–18) recall his past deeds and their enduring significance. Unlike the short lives of humans, the Lord's love endures across generations. Verse 19 is a single line of praise complementing verse 6. Together they declare his rule to be just in character and over all the earth in extent. The final stanza (vv. 20–22) calls on all—from heaven's inhabitants to the earthly creation—to praise the Lord.

SPECIAL NOTES: The statement that the Lord is "compassionate and gracious, slow to anger, abounding in love" goes back to God's forgiveness of Israel after the people made an idol in the wilderness while Moses was on Mount Sinai receiving the Law (Ex. 34:6). It is reiterated in Nehemiah 9:17; Psalms 86:15; 103:8; 145:8; Joel 2:13; and Jonah 4:2.

While not an alphabetic acrostic, the psalm has exactly twenty-two lines, the same as the number of letters in the Hebrew alphabet. This line count has been chosen for several psalms.

REFLECTION: Like a fountain bubbling over, the psalmist, in conversation with his own soul, attributes praise to God. Multiplying into a communal voice in a rising crescendo, the hymn eventually lifts us into ecstatic praise, a fitting prelude to thanksgiving sacrifice—thanks because of gratitude and awe; giving because of receiving so much.

Psalm 104

THEME: The Lord, who created the heavens and the earth and beneficially ordered them, should be feared and praised.

TYPE: Hymn of praise/thanksgiving.

AUTHOR: Unknown.

BACKGROUND: In general, the elements of creation occur in an order similar to that of Genesis 1. Several similarities (as well as differences) have been observed between Psalm 104 and literary works from Egypt, Phoenicia, and Babylon. So in terms understood throughout the nearby nations, Psalm 104 asserts that it is the Lord who is the Creator on whom all life depends.

© Bill Kennedy/www.istockphoto.com

STRUCTURE: Stanza 1 (vv. 1–4) makes a call to bless the Lord and proceeds to praise him for his majesty, using the imagery of one who dwells in the heavens and is clothed with light. Stanza 2 (vv. 5–9) demonstrates God's power by recounting how he established the earth and set boundaries for the waters. Stanza 3 (vv. 10–15) praises God for the rain he sends to provide water for animals as well as vegetation and crops. Stanza 4 (vv. 16–23) records how God has made both places and times for his creatures. Stanza 5 (vv. 24–30) continues to praise God, considering both sea and land creatures, recognizing that life and death are in his hands. In stanza 6 (vv. 31–35a) the psalmist expresses the desire that God's works endure and makes a vow to continue to praise the Lord. The rest of verse 35 closes the hymn, returning to the thought of the opening line.

SPECIAL NOTES: Psalms 8, 19, 29, and 148 also treat creation as a major theme. On God's provision of food, compare 104:27–28 with 145:15–16.

REFLECTION: Patents, proprietary processes, trademarks—what are the rights that go with making something? Copyrights, footnotes, and permissions—what are the responsibilities for giving credit where credit is due? When gifts are given, what should be the gratitude of the recipients? The Lord has designed, made, and ordered all things. While we have been granted an independence of will, we do not have an independence of existence. We have no existence apart from God's sustaining power. Our Maker deserves our praise and obedience.

Psalm 105

THEME: Remember that God remembers his covenant, just as he gave Israel the Promised Land through many mighty deeds.

TYPE: Hymn of praise/thanksgiving.

AUTHOR: Unknown.

BACKGROUND: First Chronicles 16 uses Psalm 105 when recounting the bringing of the ark of the covenant to Jerusalem. First Chronicles 16:8–22 corresponds to Psalm 105:1–15 and commemorates God's covenant with Abraham and protection of the patriarchs. First Chronicles 16:23–33 then incorporates Psalm 96, though with slight differences. Psalm 105, on the other hand, continues on to commemorate God delivering Israel from Egypt. As a historical review of God's saving work, the psalm would have been fit for many occasions in Israel's worship.

Brock, Charles Edmund (1870-1938)/Private Collection/The Bridgeman Art Library

STRUCTURE: Stanza 1 (vv. 1–4) is a general call to praise. Stanza 2 (vv. 5–7) calls on the people to remember God's miraculous judgments. Stanza 3 (vv. 8–11) begins a review of God's history of Israel by affirming that he remembers his covenant with Abraham. Stanza 4 (vv. 12–24) tells of the patriarchs until their move to Egypt under Joseph's leadership. Verse 25 is a hinge line, marking a transition in the story line, that Egypt turned against them. Stanza 5 (vv. 26–38) tells of the plagues leading up to Israel's exodus from Egypt. Stanza 6 (vv. 39–41) recalls God's care for the people in the wilderness. Closing the historical overview, stanza 7 (vv. 42–45b) affirms that God remembered his covenant by giving his people the Promised Land. Lastly, verse 45c closes the hymn, returning to the thought of the opening line.

REFLECTION: Overwhelmingly, the subject of most sentences here is God. He made a covenant with Abraham, swore an oath to Isaac, and confirmed it to Jacob as an everlasting covenant. He rebuked kings, called down famine, and destroyed all their food. He sent a man ahead and then made his people fruitful, too numerous for their foes. He commissioned Moses and Aaron, sent the plagues, and brought his people out of Egypt. He covered them, fed them, and provided water from the rock—all because he remembered his holy promise to Abraham, his servant. Why would his faithfulness have such appeal? Because at some point, everyone will disappoint us, let us down, forget. We all know the fear, doubt, and suspicion that result. But because God is faithful to his word, seek his face always, you his chosen ones; "keep his precepts and observe his laws. Praise the Lord" (v. 45).

Psalm 106

THEME: The Lord's faithfulness surpasses the historic sins of the people; may we praise him, and may he deliver us again.

TYPE: Mixed: praise, instruction, communal lament.

AUTHOR: Unknown.

BACKGROUND: The bulk of the psalm is a review of Israel's history, serving as an instructive reminder not to repeat the sins of the past. The singers take ownership of these sins and bracket this history with petitions for God to deliver, giving it characteristics of a communal lament. Finally, it is encased in a call to praise and public affirmation of praise, emphasizing God's faithfulness throughout this history.

STRUCTURE: Stanza 1 (vv. 1–3): Call to praise.

Stanza 2 (vv. 4–5): Petition for God to remember and deliver the one praying.

Stanza 3 (vv. 6–12): Confession of sin in solidarity with their ancestors and review of their rebellion and deliverance at the Red Sea in Exodus 14.

Stanza 4 (vv. 13–18): Rebellion and judgment in Numbers 16.

Stanza 5 (vv. 19–23): Idolatry in making a golden calf in Exodus 32.

Stanza 6 (vv. 24–27): Failure to take the land in Numbers 14.

Stanza 7 (vv. 28–33): Rebellion in Numbers 25 and complaining at Meribah in Numbers 20, leading to Moses' rash words.

Stanza 8 (vv. 34–38): Failure to fully take the land and entanglement with idols as in the book of Judges.

Stanza 9 (vv. 39–46): Indictment of the people for their sins.

Stanza 10 (v. 47): Petition for deliverance.

Stanza 11 (v. 48): Statement of praise.

SPECIAL NOTES: First Chronicles 16, which incorporates Psalm 105:1–15 and Psalm 96, finishes its song for bringing the ark of the covenant to Jerusalem with the opening and closing verses of Psalm 106 (1 Chron. 16:34–36 is nearly identical to Ps. 106:1, 47–48).

Luke 1:68, 71, and 72 bear similarities to Psalm 106:8, 10, and 45–46.

First Corinthians 10:6, 10, and 20 bear similarities to Psalm 106:14, 25–27, and 37.

Peter Dennis © Dorling Kindersley

REFLECTION: Repetition. How often the people repeated their sins. How often God repeated his mercy. Israel's rebellions are traced from the far past to the exile, the worst position it has been in. Is it a point of no return? The psalmist doesn't think so. He expresses ownership of sins (v. 6). Citation of ancestral sins does not shift blame but positions the current community in the tradition of that rebellion. Still, the psalm does not emphasize the people's repentance, but rather, the intervention of others and the Lord's mercy and recognition of their suffering (vv. 8, 23, 30, 44, 45). What about us or people we know when we have persisted in rebellion—when is it too late? We may face harsh measures, but as long as we are willing to repent of our sins, we can turn to God for mercy.

Psalm 107

THEME: The Lord has delivered many people from many desperate circumstances, and such deeds call us to consider his love.

TYPE: Mixed: praise, instruction.

AUTHOR: Unknown.

BACKGROUND: There is some uncertainty about the background. The different groups of people it mentions have been viewed as people scattered from the land into exile and then restored. This fits its current position in the Psalter (see the Reflection). But it may be that the psalm reflects on the continuity of the character of God's saving actions at different times and places. Note how verses 23–30 can be seen as a reflection on Jonah 1.

The return of the exiles, Hole, William Brassey/Private Collection/© Look and Learn/The Bridgeman Art Library International

STRUCTURE: The psalm opens with a call to praise (vv. 1–3) and closes with a call to ponder and understand these things (vv. 42–43). The bulk of the psalm has four episodes (vv. 4–9, 10–16, 17–22, and 23–32) that describe people in distress who call to God and are delivered. These episodes stress the theme of different circumstances but common deliverance by repeating two verses in each episode. One of the repeating verses reports that they cried to God and he answered. Then, after a unique description of how God answered, the second verse calls each group to praise God. Verses 33–41 offer general descriptions of the kinds of marvelous things God did, highlighting his power to do opposite sorts of things.

SPECIAL NOTES: It is possible that verses 39 and 40 have become reversed from their original order.

REFLECTION: Opening book 5 of the Psalter, Psalm 107 seems like a response to Psalm 106. Psalm 106 holds out the hope that God will save and "gather us from the nations" (Ps. 106:47), taking heart in the fact that Israel's long history of rebellion could be outdone by God's mercy. Psalm 107 calls for praises to God from "those he gathered from the lands" (v. 3). The stories in Psalm 107 compel us to "ponder the loving deeds of the LORD" (v. 43)—proof indeed that it is never too late to repent.

Psalm 108

THEME: Despite God's apparent lack of aid against Edom, the psalmist is determined to praise God and affirm his sovereignty over other nations.

TYPE: Communal lament.

AUTHOR: A psalm (*mizmor*) of David. A song (*shir*).

BACKGROUND: Psalm 108 combines sections from two other laments. Psalm 108:1–5 is nearly identical to Psalm 57:7–11, which is a statement of confidence closing an individual lament. Psalm 108:6–13 repeats Psalm 60:5–12 exactly. Psalm 60 differs in that it begins not with confidence but with complaint of God's rejection. Such sharing of verses between psalms is evidence that psalm material could be adapted beyond its original setting. Perhaps we should envision the king reciting verses 1–5 and the community reciting the rest of the psalm.

STRUCTURE: Stanza 1 (vv. 1–5) moves from a statement of confidence to a vow to praise and a statement of praise. Stanza 2 (vv. 6–9) begins with a petition to rescue and is followed by a prophetic word about God's reign and his favorable treatment of Israel. Stanza 3 (vv. 10–13) mixes complaint, petition, and confidence.

SPECIAL NOTES: The phrases "rejected us" and "no longer go out with our armies" are terms of abandonment (cf. Ps. 44:9). Yet the psalm opens and closes with confidence in God.

AP/Wide World Photos

REFLECTION: The psalm exhibits tension between confidence and doubt. The first individual speaker, likely the king, sounds a note of confidence. A prophetic oracle reinforces this expectation. But recent history has furnished evidence of God not being with his people in battle, introducing doubt. They do not suppress the doubt or minimize their accusation against God. Yet the community and the king cry for God to deliver, since deliverance lies solely with God. Despite the doubt, they close with a statement of confidence, as if to say, "Lord, we believe, help our unbelief."

Psalm 109

THEME: May the betrayers and false accusers receive what they desired to happen against the psalmist who befriended them; may it be clear that God has done it.

© Michael Courtney/www.istockphoto.com

TYPE: Individual lament.

AUTHOR: A psalm (*mizmor*) of David. For the director of music.

BACKGROUND: Someone from the ancient world would likely find our justice system strange. Jail time might seem more like free room and board than justice. For how does staying in jail do anything to make restitution for theft or other crimes? In the ancient Near East, justice was generally viewed as making restitution (plus fines) or receiving equal consequences. One of the Babylonian legal statements even says that false accusers and false witnesses should receive the penalty that they were trying to force on the accused. The psalmist here asks for severe penalties against his false accusers. Perhaps there is some hyperbole, but it is still likely that these were the things the false accusers wished on the psalmist.

STRUCTURE: Stanza 1 (vv. 1–5) begins with a single-line petition and proceeds to list the accusations against the psalmist's enemies. Stanza 2 (vv. 6–15) asks God to deal out harsh and enduring punishments, probably of the same character as the hateful words they have been speaking. Stanza 3 (vv. 16–25) may be divided into two halves. The first continues to focus on the enemies, with accusations and calls for punishment. The second focuses on the psalmist, with a petition and lament. Stanza 4 (vv. 26–29) petitions for help and again requests punishments on the enemies. The closing two lines promise to praise God and affirm that he helps the needy.

SPECIAL NOTES: In Acts 1:20 Peter applies Psalm 109:8 to the decision to replace Judas with another apostle. Like Judas, the enemies in Psalm 109 are those who betray friendship.

REFLECTION: Proverbs 12:7 says, "The wicked are overthrown and are no more, but the house of the righteous stands firm." Many other verses support the principle of retribution, that God delights to reward the righteous and really does punish the wicked. We often have two kinds of problems with this principle. One is making sense of the wicked prospering or the righteous suffering, as in the story of Job. The other is wrestling with the feelings that go with wanting to see justice done or hearing it requested—asking for the punishments on the guilty that match their wickedness. In both cases, they must be placed in God's hands. Job's friends needed to leave the evaluation of Job in God's hands. The psalmist, who freely expresses desired penalties for the wicked, places the punishments in God's hands and does not take them into his own.

Psalm 110

THEME: The Lord promises to make David and his kingdom secure from their enemies and elevates the king to a priestly status.

TYPE: Royal.

AUTHOR: A psalm (*mizmor*) of David.

BACKGROUND: The psalm contains prophetic oracles, but the setting is not known with certainty. Perhaps they followed David's capture of Jerusalem and are given as a promise of God continuing to grant David military success. While David could not be a priest in the Levitical order, the psalm places him in the tradition of the former king of [Jeru]Salem, Melchizedek, known from Genesis 14:18.

STRUCTURE: Stanza 1 (v. 1) is a prophetic oracle promising David (or perhaps the Davidic heir) victory over his enemies. In stanza 2 (vv. 2–3) the Lord promises to extend David's rule and remarks on the troops' willingness to follow their king in battle. In stanza 3 (v. 4) the Lord aligns David (and his heirs) with a priestly position, after the type of former priest-king Melchizedek. In the last stanza (vv. 5–7) the prophet assures the king of future victories.

SPECIAL NOTES: Psalm 110 is the psalm most quoted or referred to in the New Testament. Compare Psalm 110:1 with Mark 16:19; Romans 8:34; 1 Corinthians 15:25; Ephesians 1:20; Colossians 3:1; Hebrews 1:3; 8:1; 10:12, 13; 12:2. And compare Psalm 110:4 with John 12:34; Hebrews 5:10; 6:20; 7:3.

Pieter Lastman (1583–1633)/The Detroit Institute of Arts, USA/Founders Society purchase and Dexter M. Ferry Jr. fund. Gift of Mr. and Mrs. John N. Lord/The Bridgeman Art Library

REFLECTION: This psalm is written for the king. None of us is the king. The Lord extends the king's scepter, suppresses the king's enemies, and appoints the king to the priesthood. None of us is the king. But the king's battles are the community's battles. The community benefits from the king and God's blessings on him.

Consider the book of Ruth. There the plight of two widows is remedied by Boaz marrying Ruth and raising up offspring for the benefit even of her mother-in-law, Naomi. Not all the girls in Israel could marry Boaz. Nevertheless, everyone benefited, for the line led to David. And not everyone can be David. But everyone can benefit, for the line led to Christ. We rejoice in the blessings on the King and give our allegiance to our King and Lord. And we participate in those blessings.

Psalm 111

THEME: God has worked wonders for his people and shown covenant faithfulness; he should be honored and obeyed.

TYPE: Hymn of praise/thanksgiving.

AUTHOR: Unknown.

BACKGROUND: Psalm 111 has several vocabulary links to Exodus 34:6 and 10, which describe God as "compassionate and gracious," performing wonders and making a covenant. As verse 1 clearly envisions testifying of God's greatness in a public setting, it may have been a praise hymn sung by an individual or used with a thanksgiving offering (a type of peace offering, which is described in Lev. 3; 7:11–15; and 22:29–30). On such occasions worshipers would declare what the Lord had done for them. Psalm 111 is also intimately tied to Psalm 112.

Western Scenics

STRUCTURE: Psalms 111 and 112 are both alphabetic acrostics with the same number of syllables (in Hebrew) and an identical line structure. After an initial call to "praise the LORD," there are twenty-two line segments forming the alphabetic acrostic. They are arranged as ten poetic lines in a 1-4-4-1 pattern. The first eight lines are two-part lines (bicola), while the last two lines are three-part lines (tricola).

Line 1 of the acrostic is an invitation to hear the psalmist praise God. The next two stanzas (vv. 2–5 and 6–9) praise God for his mighty works of deliverance for the nation. Verse 10 responds to God's deeds with a wisdom saying advising one to fear and obey the Lord.

SPECIAL NOTES: The Lord is described as "compassionate and gracious" in Exodus 34:6; 2 Chronicles 30:9; Nehemiah 9:17, 31; Psalms 86:15; 103:8; 111:4; 145:8; Joel 2:13; and Jonah 4:2.

About half of the words in Psalms 111 and 112 are used in both psalms. The words that Psalm 111 uses more than once but are not in Psalm 112 are terms for "work," "wonders," "faithfulness," "to/for his people," and "covenant."

REFLECTION: Israel received many benefits from the Lord, some of which are mentioned in this psalm. God performed majestic and memorable acts. He provided food, land, and redemption. He made a lasting covenant with them. But the story is not mainly about Israel; it is about God. It is not an occasion for pride, but rather, praise—not "Look at me," but "Look at him." His works are "faithful," "righteous," "gracious," "compassionate," "just," and "trustworthy." The story is not about you or me. The story is about God and our response to him.

Psalm 112

THEME: The one who fears and obeys the Lord is compassionate and righteous, firm and without fear.

TYPE: Wisdom.

AUTHOR: Unknown.

BACKGROUND: Psalm 112 probably regularly followed Psalm 111 as if two parts of one psalm. Together they remind the community of God's redemption and illustrate the response of a proper life under his authority.

STRUCTURE: Psalm 112 and 111 are both alphabetic acrostics with the same number of syllables (in Hebrew) and an identical line structure. After an initial call to "praise the LORD," there are twenty-two line segments forming the alphabetic acrostic. They are arranged as ten poetic lines in a pattern: 1-4-4-1. The first eight lines are two-part lines (bicola), while the last two lines are three-part lines (tricola).

Line 1 of the acrostic is a blessing formula that links back to the wisdom saying ending Psalm 111. The next two stanzas (vv. 2–5 and 6–9) describe the righteous person and the kinds of blessings in the righteous person's life. Verse 10 makes a contrast, noting the displeasure of the wicked at the strength and stability of the compassionate and at the loss of their own desires.

© James Steidl/www.istockphoto.com

SPECIAL NOTES: About half of the words in Psalms 111 and 112 are used in both psalms. By this means, Psalm 112 connects the righteous person to the description of the Lord in Psalm 111. The words that Psalm 112 uses more than once but are not in Psalm 111 are terms for "man/person," "righteous," "wicked," and "seeing." These contrast the righteous and the wicked, their perspectives and their outcomes.

REFLECTION: A variation on Psalm 1, this psalm extols the blessings of the righteous—those who delight in God's commands, who are gracious and compassionate, who are just and generous and lend freely. These blessings are not just unseen, private, and personal, but observable, corporate—like a city on a hill—for the wicked see and are vexed. The wicked are distinguished not so much by a lack of health or wealth, but by their wasting away in bitterness and longing; greed and avarice mark them and eventually suck the marrow from their lives.

Not so the righteous. They are the benefactors of the earth, not hoarding blessings for gloating. "They have scattered abroad their gifts to the poor" (v. 9), and this service to the world is credited to them as righteousness, enduring forever. "Blessed are those who hunger and thirst for righteousness" (Mt. 5:6).

Psalm 113

THEME The Lord is great enough to reign over all peoples and humble enough to help the needy of society.

© Steve Debenport/www.istockphoto.com

TYPE: Hymn of praise.

AUTHOR: Unknown.

BACKGROUND: This psalm was probably intended for a public ceremony but is so generic in its praise that it would be suitable for many occasions.

STRUCTURE: Two stanzas are sandwiched by two calls to praise the Lord. Stanza 1 (vv. 1–4) is a call to praise and a statement of praise emphasizing that he is Lord everywhere. Stanza 2 (vv. 5–9) is one long sentence in Hebrew. It is a rhetorical question asserting that there is none like the Lord. It lists both his characteristics of glory and his attention to the needy of society. Verse 5 is at the center of the psalm, asserting the Lord's kingship.

SPECIAL NOTES: "From the rising of the sun . . ." (v. 3) is a geographic reference. The Lord reigns from the east to the west. The common thinking of the surrounding nations is that gods had certain associations, perhaps with a certain power seen in nature, or in relationship to a country, specifically to the portion of land (rather than the people). In contrast the Lord makes it clear that he is committed to his people and rules over all countries and nations.

Characterizing God as one who helps the poor, needy, and barren may remind us of issues of social mercy and justice. It is important to remember that these should be distinguished from the foolish and lazy who are not portrayed positively in Proverbs.

REFLECTION: "Power corrupts and absolute power corrupts absolutely." Or so we know it is with us humans. How easy it is to think that rank has its privileges more so than its responsibilities. How easy to think of ourselves more highly than we ought to (Rom. 12:3). But what of he who should be praised from east to west, enthroned above both earth and heaven? He rescues the poor and needy and attends to the woman struggling with infertility. One of the great purposes of power is to help the weak (Phil. 2:1–11).

Psalm 114

THEME: Be in awe of the God who dominated the waters when he brought Israel out of Egypt.

TYPE: Hymn of praise/thanksgiving.

AUTHOR: Unknown.

BACKGROUND: Psalm 114 celebrates the exodus from Egypt (Ex. 14) and God's provision of water in the wilderness (Ex. 17:6; Num. 20:8; cf. Deut. 8:15). The psalm groups together the parting of the Red Sea under Moses (Ex. 14:21–26) and the stopping of the Jordan under Joshua (Josh. 3:14–17). The psalm emphasizes God's authority over water in various forms. It asserts his power against Egyptian and Canaanite beliefs in their gods associated with water in sea, river, or rain.

Calling on the name of Jehovah, Brock, Charles Edmund (1870-1938)/ Private Collection/The Bridgeman Art Library International

STRUCTURE: The psalm has four stanzas of two lines each. The first stanza (vv. 1–2) sets the stage, the exodus from Egypt as part of God making a people for himself. The second and third stanzas (vv. 3–4 and 5–6) look at God's impact on nature. The second stanza describes the events, while the third asks rhetorically, "Why?" The fourth stanza (vv. 7–8) answers the rhetorical question with the instruction for the earth to tremble before Jacob's God.

SPECIAL NOTES: Jacob was renamed as Israel (Gen. 32:28), but both names appear in this psalm. Since the nation divided into two kingdoms (called Israel and Judah), the name Jacob is a way to refer to the two kingdoms as a unity.

REFLECTION: Waterfalls, riptides, tsunamis, flash floods, cold lakes—water is powerful and can be very dangerous. Those who live near or boat on the ocean or the Great Lakes learn to respect the water, as do those who live in flash-flood regions when it rains and those who live near rivers when they swell with melting snow. If a levee breaches, you don't stand in the way of the water. So what, or rather who, can turn the waters back and can make the mountains skip like rams? God proved himself at the Red Sea and at the Jordan. Is there anything the Lord cannot do? Tremble indeed at his presence.

Psalm 115

THEME: Trust in the Lord, who is not a dead idol but rules in heaven and blesses his people.

TYPE: Mixed: instruction, praise.

AUTHOR: Unknown.

BACKGROUND: Similar passages in Isaiah suggest a possible setting, even if not the actual historical background. If ever the enemies of Israel were victorious, as under the punishments forecast by Isaiah, their foes might taunt them, claiming their own gods were superior to Israel's Lord. This psalm admonishes Israel to trust the Lord and not consider foreign gods. But the message would speak powerfully to any setting where the ways of nonbelievers seem attractive for a time.

© Kim Zeilstra/Zondervan

STRUCTURE: Psalm 115 has three main sections arranged symmetrically as eight lines, three lines, and eight more lines. Section 1 (vv. 1–8) directs glory to God by contrasting the dead idols of surrounding nations with the God of heaven who does as he pleases. The center three lines (vv. 9–11) call the people to trust in the Lord. The last eight lines (vv. 12–18) express confidence in the Lord's blessing.

SPECIAL NOTES: Psalm 115:4–11 and Psalm 135:15–20 are nearly identical. The main thought is also emphasized in Isaiah 37:19; 44:6–20; 45:11–25; Jeremiah 10:1–16; and Revelation 9:20.

The Lord's name occurs ten times.

REFLECTION: "You shall have no other gods before me." Is there really any choice? "There is no other God apart from me," says the Lord in Isaiah 45:21. The category of "God" has only one member. There are other life forms: plants, animals, humans, and even angels and demons. But no other gods. The existence of all beings is sustained by him, even those who oppose him. God prizes free will and allows his creatures to pretend he can be ignored or to choose to position themselves against him. And his mercy may allow this opposition to continue for a time. But all such opposition, be it from the human or angelic realm, has no actual power to oppose him. The lies are abundant: that idols represent other gods, that random chance alone produced the ecosystems we live in, that there is no absolute truth, that it is most important to be liked and be like those around us. But they are just lies and fake choices, not real options. There may be other challengers, but God has no actual competitor. There is no other God.

Psalm 116

THEME: The psalmist praises God for deliverance from death.

TYPE: Hymn of thanksgiving.

AUTHOR: Unknown.

BACKGROUND: This psalm seems to be the type of psalm one might sing after praying a lament and then being delivered by God. The psalmist refers back to being rescued by God though having felt threatened with death.

STRUCTURE: In stanza 1 (vv. 1–2) the psalmist affirms that God has listened in what is described as a life-threatening situation in stanza 2 (vv. 3–4). Stanza 3 (vv. 5–6) praises God's character as a protector. Therefore the singer calls his own soul to rest in verse 7 before continuing to praise God in verses 8–9.

The first stanza of the second half (vv. 10–11) recounts how the psalmist turned to God in distress. Then in verse 12 the psalmist asks, using several words from verse 7, how the Lord's kindness can be repaid. The next three stanzas (vv. 13–14, 15–16, and 17–19) make promises to God and affirm confidence in his care. The second-to-last stanza (vv. 15–16) mirrors the psalm's second stanza (vv. 3–4) in presenting the danger of death.

SPECIAL NOTES: The phrase "walk before the LORD" in verse 9 carries the sense of living a morally responsible life before God.

REFLECTION: The psalmist sings to the congregation, to the Lord, to his own soul, and to the city of Jerusalem, a tribute to God and his deliverance from death. Interestingly, the description of this tribute is "lifting up the cup of salvation." "What shall I return to the LORD for all his goodness to me? I will lift up the cup of salvation and call on the name of the LORD" (vv. 12, 13). Simply receiving what has been given, the psalmist lifts it up and drinks—a cup overflowing with goodness and mercy, grace and compassion. This is his return, to simply drink what he is thirstiest for, to receive what he most longs to be given. "Taste and see that the LORD is good" (Ps. 34:8).

Psalm 117

THEME: All peoples should praise the Lord because of his care for his people.

TYPE: Hymn of praise.

AUTHOR: Unknown.

BACKGROUND: Serving as a call to praise, this psalm may have been used prior to other psalms of praise or the sharing of praise and thanks among worshipers.

STRUCTURE: This brief psalm has only one stanza. It ends a group of psalms beginning with 111 that begin or end with the phrase "Praise the LORD."

SPECIAL NOTES: The psalm encapsulates two important notions of Israel's theology: (1) the Lord is God over all nations (not just one), and (2) the Lord is related to a people (not merely to a land).

REFLECTION: Like an extended coda sung by a great choir at peak volume, the grand theme "Praise the LORD" brackets "Great is his love toward us," thus closing out these hymns of praise. A fitting end!

Psalm 118

THEME: When coming to worship, the psalmist gives a testimony of praise for how God delivered from many enemies, turning the situation around to give victory.

TYPE: Liturgy, praise/thanksgiving.

AUTHOR: Unknown.

BACKGROUND: The picture of first being surrounded by the nations as opponents and later of victory shouts suggests that thanks are being given after a battle. It is reasonable then, but not necessary, to envision the king speaking on behalf of the army.

The different speaking voices reveal the liturgical element of Psalm 118. The call to the community to praise God is followed by the testimony of an individual. Near the end of the testimony, the community responds. The individual's call to open the gates (v. 19) and the community's reference to a procession and to the altar (v. 27) suggest a celebration, such as a feast day. Verse 26 is quoted by the crowds when Jesus came to Jerusalem for the Passover (Matt. 21:9; Mark 11:9; John 12:13).

STRUCTURE: The first and last verses are the same, providing a frame for the psalm calling for praise to God. The first stanza (vv. 2–4) calls the community to praise, affirming that the Lord's love endures forever. An individual begins to give testimony to that fact in stanza 2 (vv. 5–7). The next two seven-line stanzas (vv. 8–14 and 15–21) develop two themes from stanza 2: crying to the Lord in distress and having victory. The community probably speaks verse 20. In stanzas 5 and 6 (vv. 22–24 and 25–27) the community expresses awed praise for the Lord's deliverance and petitions God for success and blessing on the one who comes in the name of the Lord. Verse 28 provides one more line for the individual speaker, possibly the king, to affirm his loyalty to God.

SPECIAL NOTES: The Lord's name occurs seven times each in stanzas 3 and 4, seven times in stanzas 5 and 6, and seven more times besides.

Psalm 118:22 is quoted in Matthew 21:42; Mark 12:10; Luke 20:17; and 1 Peter 2:7. It is also interpreted in Acts 4:11.

Psalm 118:6 is echoed in Romans 8:31; both are in contexts of triumph amid opposition. Psalm 118:20 is echoed in John 10:9.

REFLECTION: The rejected stone becomes the capstone. How often it might be said that "God chose the foolish things of the world to shame the wise; God chose the weak things of the world to shame the strong" (1 Cor. 1:27). He does great and unexpected things. These precious benefits for the individual and community come all by God's grace.

Psalm 119

THEME: The Lord's praiseworthy laws guide, protect, enrich, and enable life; ponder his word deeply and often.

TYPE: Wisdom.

AUTHOR: Unknown.

STRUCTURE: This psalm is an alphabetic acrostic with twenty-two sections of eight verses. Each of the eight verses in a section begins with the same letter of the Hebrew alphabet. The topic of every stanza is God's "law," or "instruction."

Paul Venning

SPECIAL NOTES: This long psalm begins with a reference to a blameless life (v. 1), which is also referred to in Psalms 15:2; 26:1, 11; 84:11; and 101:2, 6.

First John 2:10 seems to echo Psalm 119:165, interpreting the essence of the "law" as the requirement to love one's neighbor as oneself.

Revelation 16:5 and 7 seem to echo Psalm 119:137.

The Hebrew word often translated "heart" also means "mind." The psalm recommends pondering, memorizing, recalling, and in other ways thinking about God's Word. These are activities related to the mind. Ancient Israel did not make a distinction between "head knowledge" and "heart knowledge." Rather, it distinguished between those who truly obeyed God and those who honored God with their lips but whose minds/hearts were far from him. Choosing to have God's Word "on your mind" is an essential part of taking it into your "heart."

REFLECTION: Presenting 176 thoughts about God's Word, this psalm is a monument to the central place God's Word should have in life—that truly we "do not live on bread alone, but on every word that comes from the mouth of God" (Mt. 4:4). Many of the thoughts in this poem can be grouped into certain categories. Using words like "precious," "delight," "desire," and "hope," the psalmist expresses how highly God's Word is valued. Its benefits include protection, freedom, stability, and life. These are thoroughly interwoven with the guidance, direction, and wisdom derived from God's Word. But that comes only through a process of committed contemplation and meditation. It was and is no small thing to break from the surrounding unbiblical views of the world and adopt the ways and values taught in God's Word. Here the psalmist finds nothing more practical than thinking about God's teachings and examining daily life and motives. Beyond finding applications in God's Word for our lives, the psalmist would have us apply our lives to God's Word. Therein the psalmist develops purity and righteous character and experiences the benefits of following the Word of the Lord.

Psalm 120

© Roy Morsch/CORBIS

THEME: May God deliver from lies and punish the liars.

TYPE: Individual lament.

AUTHOR: Unknown. A song (*shir*) of ascents.

BACKGROUND: The psalmist appears to be outside the land of Israel, which makes it difficult to place the circumstances that lie behind it. While David was sometimes outside Israel when on the run from Saul, we are not told that he visited the places mentioned in the psalm. That Isaiah, Jeremiah, and Ezekiel mention the places in the psalm might suggest that the speaker is a prophet who has to deal with false prophets. Ezekiel's ministry was outside of Israel. But Jeremiah also addresses false prophets among the Jews in Babylon in Jeremiah 29. There he advises the people to settle and marry and pray for the well-being of the city they live in, rather than advocate or expect a speedy return. It would also have been easy to apply this psalm in the time of Esther.

STRUCTURE: There are three stanzas. Stanza 1 (vv. 1–2) gives the psalmist's petition. The rhetorical question and answer in stanza 2 (vv. 3–4) acts as an imprecation, calling for punishment on the deceitful. In stanza 3 (vv. 5–7) the psalmist laments being stuck among people bent on war rather than peace.

SPECIAL NOTES: The lying tongue is sometimes compared to a weapon, such as a sword or arrow (Pss. 57:4; 64:3; Jer. 9:8). This may motivate the image of using arrows as punishment for the deceitful tongue in verses 3–4.

The places Kedar and Meshek are also mentioned in Isaiah (chaps. 60 and 66), Jeremiah (chaps. 2 and 49), and Ezekiel (chaps. 27, 32, 38, and 39). Kedar is to the east of the Jordan River. The location of Meshek is uncertain.

REFLECTION: The individual lament does not have to arise from a life-or-death situation. This psalm gives voice to distress that does not involve impending doom. The psalmist is removed from the homeland, from access to Jerusalem. Not only is he experiencing culture shock, but the people around him are antagonistic. The psalmist feels hemmed in and pushed away from peace. The forces in play are beyond his control. The only thing to do is appeal to the Lord. What may sound like "venting" at the end of the psalm serves both to release angst and to align himself with the desires of God. Lamenting is not simply going on a rant in God's presence.

Psalm 121

THEME: The Lord constantly protects the one who trusts in him.

TYPE: Confidence, possibly royal.

AUTHOR: Unknown. A song (*shir*) of ascents.

BACKGROUND: Psalm 121 shares several similarities with Psalm 91, most notably that one person professes confidence in the Lord and another pronounces God's protection. If Psalm 91 is royal, then Psalm 121 may be royal as well. Such assurances may sound unconditional and eternal but are dependent on the beginning premise of the speaker's allegiance to the Lord.

STRUCTURE: Four stanzas of two lines each make up Psalm 121, with each stanza expressing confidence in God. In the first stanza (vv. 1–2), the speaker, who may be the king, expresses both commitment to and confidence in the Lord. The next three stanzas (vv. 3–4, 5–6, and 7–8) have a different speaking voice. Here a priestly or prophetic voice speaks assurance of the Lord's protection.

SPECIAL NOTES: The promise in verse 3 is similar to that of Psalm 91:12.

The first stanza connects the hills and the Lord as a source of help. Obviously hills do not act. But Mount Zion, the Lord's earthly dwelling, is set in the hill country, and God's home is in heaven. So the Lord is sometimes pictured as coming like a warrior/rescuer to hills around Zion. A related picture is also expressed in Psalm 125:2 (also cf. Ps. 123:1). When looking toward the hills, the psalmist is looking for the Lord.

"Shade" does not simply mean a shadow or the result of something blocking the sun's rays. It is a picture of shielding protection.

REFLECTION: This psalm talks about two watchings: the psalmist lifting up his eyes to God and God watching over the psalmist. One needs help and looks up; the other, looking down, gives help. Both offer their faces in relationship—ascending and descending, coming and going, forevermore. Watching is a great metaphor for relationship.

Psalm **122**

THEME: It is a joy to go to Jerusalem to worship at the Lord's house; may the city be blessed with peace.

TYPE: Zion song; pilgrimage.

AUTHOR: Of David. A song (*shir*) of ascents.

BACKGROUND: Verse 4 remarks that it is a statute to go to Jerusalem to praise the Lord. Such regulations occur in Deuteronomy 12; 14:23; 16:2, 11; 26:2.

STRUCTURE: In stanza 1 (vv. 1–2) the psalmist receives an invitation to visit the Lord's house. In stanza 2 (vv. 3–5) the psalmist praises Jerusalem as a worship center and place of justice. In stanza 3 (vv. 6–9) the psalmist calls the community to pray for the well-being of the city and commits to seeking its prosperity.

SPECIAL NOTES: Jerusalem being a city "closely compacted together" may refer to its level of organization as opposed to a tribal style of arrangement that was looser and less space efficient.

Z. Radovan/www.BibleLandPictures.com

REFLECTION: Some places feel special to us—perhaps because of natural beauty and grandeur, like the Grand Canyon; perhaps because of human design, like great cathedrals, skyscrapers, or stadiums; perhaps because of nostalgia, historic events, or special memories we associate with a place. Such was Jerusalem—a city on a mountain, with the temple of the Lord, where worshipers came to celebrate regular festivals. Such is Jerusalem. Pray for the peace of Jerusalem.

Psalm 123

THEME: The people look expectantly to God for help and relief from the contempt of others.

TYPE: Communal lament.

AUTHOR: Unknown. A song (*shir*) of ascents.

BACKGROUND: The change in speaking voices from singular (v. 1) to plural (vv. 2–4) suggests a liturgical setting in which the leader is joined in prayer by the congregation.

STRUCTURE: Verse 1 affirms confidence and dependence on the Lord stated by an individual. Verse 2 expands on the imagery of looking dependently to the Lord, now spoken by the community. Finally, in verses 3–4, the community petitions the Lord for help in light of how it has been mistreated.

SPECIAL NOTES: Like Psalm 123:1, Psalm 121:1 also uses the imagery of lifting the eyes in expectation of help.

REFLECTION: This short psalm does an excellent job of showcasing the essence of lament. There is complaint but not a complaining attitude. Distress is not processed to lead to grumbling, whining, murmuring and disputing, like the Israelites in the wilderness. Yet the complaint is not done away with by belief, not swept under a theological carpet, not suppressed. It is voiced—to God himself. Not with an angry shaking of the fist, but rather, with the submission of a servant and the expectation of a hearing grounded in a mutual relationship. So let us lift our eyes to God.

Psalm 124

THEME: Praise God, and him alone, for thwarting our enemies from overwhelming us.

TYPE: Hymn of thanksgiving.

AUTHOR: Of David. A song (*shir*) of ascents.

BACKGROUND: This psalm was for occasions of praise after the Lord had delivered. The material that could have made up a lament during hardship is reported here as a "would have been." The threat from enemies had been real and significant, but God had prevented it.

STRUCTURE: The psalm has two stanzas. Stanza 1 (vv. 1–5) praises God for deliverance by saying what would have been if God had not been for his people. Stanza 2 (vv. 6–8) praises the Lord for their escape from danger.

SPECIAL NOTES: Psalm 124:8 is very similar to Psalm 121:2.

REFLECTION: "If not for ..." Some results depend on many people and depend on them somewhat evenly. Recognition and thanks are due all around. But sometimes one person stands out: the sports star who makes spectacular plays, a quick-thinking emergency rescue worker, a pioneering inventor, a soldier or officer who makes a key decision or takes singularly brave action. Here Israel recognizes its utter dependence on God for its deliverance.

Remember the story of Gideon. God rescued Israel from Midian with three hundred men after sending away thousands. God told Gideon that there were too many people and that they might boast that they delivered themselves by their own power (Judg. 7:2, 4). The issues of pride and dependence and God's glory repeat often through Israel's history and our own lives. This psalm puts thankful humility to words to guide our thinking.

Psalm 125

© Dor Jordan/www.istockphoto.com

THEME: The Lord protects those who trust him and will deliver them from the wicked.

TYPE: Confidence.

AUTHOR: Unknown. A song (*shir*) of ascents.

BACKGROUND: The reference to the "scepter of the wicked" suggests some sort of enemy occupation of the land, though not necessarily that of the exile.

STRUCTURE: Psalm 125 has three stanzas plus a concluding line wishing blessing on Israel. Stanza 1 (vv. 1–2) is a statement of confidence that also serves as instruction to continue to trust the Lord. The second stanza (v. 3) continues to express confidence in God, though it seems to incorporate a complaint. Stanza 3 (vv. 4–5) moves on to petition in favor of those who do good and against those who are crooked.

SPECIAL NOTES: Psalms 123 and 125 are similar in that they begin with a statement of confidence, conclude with a petition for God to help, and refer briefly to elements of complaint or lament. Thus they are somewhat mixed in their type, having elements of lament as well as a hymn of confidence. Psalm 123 emphasizes the lament element more and Psalm 125 the confidence element.

REFLECTION: Confidence in contrasting circumstances. We may easily feel confidence when things are going right, when they are in our favor, when we are the victors at the top of our game. The more things that are not right, the harder it is to have confidence. In fact, it may be appropriate to lament. With the scepter of the wicked in the land, it sounds like Israel is "losing." But the psalmist is confident that it is not the end of the game. God is with his people as sure and as strong as the mountains around Jerusalem. This is the most enduring truth, not the scepter of the wicked. In this temporary chapter of the national story, individuals face a choice in their personal story. Will they be upright or turn to crooked ways? The first comes from the hope of confidence, the second from despair. The psalmist asks God that the next part of the story be the individuals getting paid back for their choices. The question for us is where our own choices lead.

Psalm 126

THEME: The Lord did great things to restore Jerusalem in the past; may he so act to restore Jerusalem again.

TYPE: Communal lament.

AUTHOR: Unknown. A song (*shir*) of ascents.

STRUCTURE: The psalm has two stanzas of four lines each. Stanza 1 (vv. 1–3) praises God for a past deliverance of Jerusalem. Stanza 2 (vv. 4–6) petitions the Lord to do so again.

SPECIAL NOTES: The Negev (v. 4) is the arid portion of country in the southern part of Judah. The idea of streams of water in the normally dry Negev creates a picture of reversal of fortunes, as does the following picture of sowing with tears but reaping with joy.

On the restoration of Zion and turning weeping to joy, see Isaiah 52:1–10 and Jeremiah 31:1–14.

REFLECTION: There is a balance in life between lament and praise. This psalm captures one dimension of the relationship between the two: "Those who go out weeping, carrying seed to sow, will return with songs of joy" (v. 6). Just as sowing precedes reaping by necessity, so too lament—an honest appraisal of one's need and situation—necessarily precedes praise. And when deliverance or restoration has finally come, it erupts as joyous laughter and praise. Perhaps the absence of hope and joy, then, suggests the possibility of a lack of lament and an honest look at one's own despair. How might our laments, then, actually enhance our praise?

Psalm 127

Kim Steele/PhotoDisc

THEME: Our security is ultimately in the Lord's hands and not our own efforts.

TYPE: Wisdom.

AUTHOR: Of Solomon. A song (*shir*) of ascents.

BACKGROUND: The psalm is more like a pair of proverbs than a typical wisdom psalm. The general reference to the "city" is probably made to refer specifically to Jerusalem in the context of being included with the psalms of "ascents."

The vocabulary of the psalm provides several links to Solomon. Solomon was responsible for building the Lord's house (1 Kings 5–8). "City" is applied to Jerusalem, the royal city. The Lord loved Solomon, who was also named Jedidiah (2 Sam. 12:24–25), which is formed from the same Hebrew root as the reference to those he loves at the end of Psalm 127:2. Solomon also had many sons, the topic of the second wisdom saying. But perhaps more significantly, Solomon represents the first of the seed, or sons, of David in the Lord's promise to build David a house (2 Sam. 7), meaning a dynasty, with his sons to sit on his throne.

STRUCTURE: The psalm has two stanzas of four lines each. Stanza 1 (vv. 1–2) concerns some of the basic efforts in life of securing food, housing, and safety. These cannot be secured strictly by personal effort but depend on the Lord. Stanza 2 (vv. 3–5) remarks on the blessings of having children.

SPECIAL NOTES: Contending with enemies in the gate is not necessarily a military reference. The city gate would also be the place of business transactions and court proceedings.

Psalm 128 is also a wisdom psalm having two stanzas of four lines. In the reverse order of the topics in Psalm 127, Psalm 128 deals with the blessing of children in the first half and with Jerusalem in the second half.

REFLECTION: Rugged individualism. It's how the West was won. It's one of the deep values in certain strands of American culture. Hard work is certainly valued in Scripture, especially in Proverbs. So it's not that it's wrong to work toward self-sufficiency. It's just that it isn't true. Ultimately, the value of the work is in God's hands. Where Proverbs rebukes the sluggard on one end of the spectrum, this psalm affirms that anxious toil is vain.

Psalm 128

THEME: To fear the Lord is the key to blessing in family and country.

TYPE: Wisdom.

AUTHOR: Unknown. A song (*shir*) of ascents.

BACKGROUND: The shift from third-person statements (vv. 1, 4) to second-person address (vv. 2–3, 5–6) suggests a ceremonial setting. The blessing statements might be made either as worshipers arrive or depart.

STRUCTURE: The psalm has two stanzas of four lines. Each begins with a third-person wisdom saying about those who fear the Lord, then proceeds to blessing statements in the second person. Stanza 1 (vv. 1–3) attributes family blessings to the one who fears the Lord. Stanza 2 (vv. 4–6) calls for the Lord to bless from Zion.

SPECIAL NOTES: Psalm 127 is also a wisdom psalm having two stanzas of four lines. The Hebrew in each of the four stanzas is essentially the same length. In the reverse order of the topics in Psalm 127, Psalm 128 deals with the blessing of children in the first half and with Jerusalem in the second half.

Z. Radovan/www.BibleLandPictures.com

REFLECTION: The blessings pronounced in this psalm echo God's design in Genesis 1–2. In the perfection of God's original design, he gave several commands. Adam and Eve were to subdue the earth and rule its creatures, as well as tend the garden of Eden (Gen. 1:26, 28; 2:15). Work was not toil but a means for expressing creativity and order. The soil and plant kingdom lacked the resistance of the curse. Only later would humankind eat by the sweat of the brow and eventually return to dust (Gen. 3:17–19). Further, they were to be fruitful and multiply (Gen. 1:28). The curse mentions pain in childbirth, but we see also that in the ancient world, childbirth was not infrequently the occasion of death. This psalm locates the blessings received by God-fearers in the same basic realms of life: work, sustenance, and family. God wants his people to be able to live from the fruit of their own labor and parents to enjoy many children. It is not the end of the curse but is an alleviation of its application. Simple joys with the fear of God are a good formula for life (cf. Eccl. 5:18; 9:9; 11:9; 12:13–14).

Psalm 129

© Ahikam Seri/www.panos.co.uk

THEME: As God has freed Jerusalem in the past, may Jerusalem's enemies be devastated.

TYPE: Communal lament or confidence.

AUTHOR: Unknown. A song (*shir*) of ascents.

BACKGROUND: The background and setting of Psalm 129 are difficult to determine. Though the psalm does not have an actual lament section, it seems closest to a lament because communal laments often include elements of praise first, and the petition to defend Jerusalem suggests danger. But it may also be viewed as a general reflection on God's past deliverance and a prayer for continued defense. In such a case, it would be more akin to a psalm of confidence. Like many of the psalms of ascents (Pss. 120–134), it deals with Zion. And it may be that the individual speaker in the first stanza is a personified Jerusalem.

STRUCTURE: The psalm has two stanzas of four lines plus a concluding line of blessing. In stanza 1 (vv. 1–4) the speaker testifies that past oppression has not meant defeat; rather, God has delivered. Stanza 2 (vv. 5–8) is a petition against those who hate Jerusalem, that they be devastated like a dry, withered field. In conclusion the community blesses the first speaker.

SPECIAL NOTES: Withering grass pictures the short life of humanity in general, or of the wicked, in several passages: Psalms 37:2; 102:4, 11; 129:6; Isaiah 15:6; 40:7–8; James 1:11; 1 Peter 1:24.

REFLECTION: Sometimes when we fall down we hop back up, but sometimes we feel like we cannot move. Here Israel says, "I've been knocked down over and over but not knocked out." Down, but not out. Is this then the pride of self-sufficiency? No. It is dependence; it comes from the recognition that the Lord has "cut me free" and stands by me. This resilience and blessing comes from another source—not from self but from the Lord. Participating in it brings hope and confidence, while the closing imprecation calls for the opposite, for shame and not blessing, on the opponents of the Lord.

Psalm 130

THEME: The psalmist, in need of forgiveness, demonstrates reliance and trust in the Lord and receives assurance.

TYPE: Mixed: lament, instruction.

AUTHOR: Unknown. A song (*shir*) of ascents.

BACKGROUND: The first three stanzas (vv. 1–6) contain an individual's lament. Then another voice speaks in verses 7–8, addressing the community. Both the individual's prayer and the following pronouncement concern forgiveness. These factors suggest that the psalm was used when bringing a sacrifice for forgiveness. The psalmist seeks forgiveness with a clear attitude of dependency yet waits confidently for the Lord. Then a priest speaks confidently, with assurance to all those who have likewise assembled. The individual's hopes are then realized as a member of the community.

STRUCTURE: Psalm 130 has four stanzas of two lines each. Stanza 1 (vv. 1–2) is the psalmist's initial appeal to be heard. Stanza 2 (vv. 3–4) makes a general confession of sin and affirms the hope of God's forgiving character. Stanza 3 (vv. 5–6) is a statement of confidence, evidenced in waiting for the Lord. Stanza 4 (vv. 7–8) is a priestly pronouncement of assurance.

REFLECTION: Are we casual about sin and accustomed to forgiveness? Do we feel entitled to receive grace? "What a wretched man I am!" says Paul (Rom. 7:24). "I do not understand what I do. For what I want to do, I do not do. But what I hate I do" (7:15). Forgiveness should not inspire a sense of entitlement; it should fill us with the fear of the Lord (Ps. 130:4). The more we recognize the wretched hopelessness of our sinning, the more we appreciate the grace we receive. And those who know they are forgiven most will love the most (cf. Luke 7:40–50).

Psalm 131

THEME: The Lord should be approached with humility and hope.

TYPE: Liturgy, instruction.

AUTHOR: Of David. A song (*shir*) of ascents.

BACKGROUND: Psalm 131 bears some similarities to Psalms 15 and 24, which are liturgies used when entering the temple area or the holy city of Jerusalem. They proclaim the proper attitude or righteous status of the worshiper. The title "Of David" may have been misplaced from Psalm 132, which is not so titled but is clearly Davidic. Or if Psalm 131 is royal, it may have been put next to Psalm 132 to represent the king's humble attitude. On the other hand, it continues the attitude of dependency and waiting of Psalm 130.

STRUCTURE: Stanza 1 (vv. 1–2) has four lines in which the psalmist declares humility and contentment in the Lord. The final line (v. 3) admonishes the community to hope in the Lord.

SPECIAL NOTES: Under the perspective that this is part of a royal liturgy, it is helpful to note the contrasting pride of King Uzziah in 2 Chronicles 26:16–21.

The perspective of waiting can be compared with Psalm 37:7.

The priestly admonition in verse 3 is similar to that of Psalm 130:7.

REFLECTION: It is easy to suppose that we know things that we do not. Evaluating other people's parenting, acting as an armchair quarterback, or prognosticating about the economy and politics is easy. People in power positions, such as a king or congresspperson, may be even more susceptible to feelings of superiority. They may think that rank has more privileges than responsibilities. But before God we are equal, and the wise person is humble, not considering himself or herself more highly than he or she should (Rom. 12:3; Phil. 2:1–5). The wise person does not even consider ranking fellow humans according to race, social position, or gender (Gal. 3:28). Our place is to know our ranking before God and to be still and know that he is in charge.

Psalm 132

THEME: The Lord blesses Jerusalem for the sake of his covenant with David.

TYPE: Mixed: royal; Zion song.

AUTHOR: Unknown. A song (*shir*) of ascents.

BACKGROUND: God makes a covenant with David in 2 Samuel 7. There God reminds him of how he has given him rest from his enemies and promises that one of David's sons will reign after him and build the temple. The Lord will establish his kingdom and be like a father to him, correcting him for his sins but staying faithful in love. In this psalm, the Davidic heir positions himself in the legacy of the Davidic covenant.

David refers to his hard work in preparing for the temple in 1 Chronicles 22:14 in a way that sounds similar to the hardships mentioned in Psalm 132:1. Solomon's prayer at the dedication of the temple in 2 Chronicles 6:41–42 echoes (or is echoed by) verses 8–10 of the psalm.

STRUCTURE: Specific mention of David in verses 1, 10, and 17 divides the psalm into its major sections. Verses 1 and 10 are petitions, and verses 17–18 are an answering promise. Verses 2–9 and 11–16 each divide further into two sets of four two-part lines (bicola; vv. 2–5, 6–9, 11–12, and 13–16). Each of these has a quotation for the last three lines. The introduction to the quotes establishes the basic flow of thought. David swore an oath to the Lord (v. 2). The people heard an invitation to worship (v. 6). The Lord swore an oath to David (v. 11a). The Lord chose Zion (v. 13). These verses position the promises between David and the Lord as embracing the community and its worship at his dwelling place in Jerusalem.

Z. Radovan/www.BibleLandPictures.com

SPECIAL NOTES: The lamp in verse 17 is a metaphor for David's heirs. When God describes splitting the kingdom into Israel and Judah, 1 Kings 11:36 refers to Judah as a place where David would have a lamp before God.

REFLECTION: This psalm beautifully models in structure the conversational nature of a relationship with God: the mutual declaring of oaths between David and the Lord; the people taking up the words of the oaths and remembering as they journey to a time of communal worship; God's faithful people asking that they might sing for joy; and the Lord allowing his people to receive the benefits of his promises to David. All this and more, ending in adoration of the king whose head is adorned with a resplendent crown.

What a glorious picture this is of life itself as we journey along, the recipients of an amazing salvation that comes to us through a historical conversation between Jesus, the ultimate Davidic heir, and his Father—all because the Lord has chosen it, desired it, and declared it: "I will bless . . . I will satisfy . . . I will clothe . . . and her faithful people will ever sing for joy" (vv. 15–16). Hallelujah!

Psalm 133

THEME: Blessing descends from God on Zion for people who dwell in unity.

TYPE: Mixed: Zion song, instruction.

AUTHOR: Of David. A song (*shir*) of ascents.

BACKGROUND: The classification and setting of the psalm are difficult to determine due to the psalm's brevity and some questions about its meaning. The "brothers" mentioned in verse 1 (NIV) may be brothers, the sons of one father, but the term can refer to relatives more broadly. Thus it may refer to the assembled worshipers of the children of Israel or to the peoples of the divided kingdoms of Israel and Judah, even after the fall of the northern kingdom of Israel. The references to Aaron's beard and to Zion suggest that the people are assembled for worship and priests are present, while the oil suggests a ceremony involving anointing. (For the anointing of Aaron himself, see Ex. 29:7 and Lev. 8:12.)

© Pete Collins/www.istockphoto.com

STRUCTURE: Verse 1 extols unity among relatives. Verses 2–3a compare the goodness of such a unity to that of the special oil used to ceremonially anoint a priest. It further uses the picture of liquid descending as a comparison with the dew on Zion. The last line, verse 3b, links back to Zion, proclaiming it to be the place where the Lord bestows blessing.

SPECIAL NOTES: Mount Hermon is a prominent mountain on the northern border of Israel.

REFLECTION: Unity is the greatest evidence of the incarnation and witness of God's love. In the hours before his crucifixion, Jesus prayed, "I have given them [his disciples] the glory that you gave me, that they may be one as we are one ... that they may be brought to complete unity. Then the world will know that you sent me and have loved them even as you have loved me" (John 17:22–23). Unity is also the mystery of God's will: "He made known to us the mystery of his will ... to bring unity to all things in heaven and on earth under Christ" (Eph. 1:9–10). Unity—like precious oil indeed, poured out on the head and running down, dripping onto our hearts—a holy anointing.

Psalm 134

THEME: Praise the Lord while serving at his house.

TYPE: Liturgy, hymn of praise.

AUTHOR: Unknown. A song (*shir*) of ascents.

BACKGROUND: There are two possible settings for this brief psalm. At the beginning of the psalm, either the priests call the assembled worshipers to praise, or more likely, departing worshipers leave with an admonition to the priests and Levites to praise God in the conduct of their duties. In either case, the importance of Zion as the source of blessing is emphasized in the concluding benediction.

STRUCTURE: Verses 1–2 are a call to praise. Verse 3 is a priestly blessing for the people.

SPECIAL NOTES: Psalm 134 ends the section of the songs of ascents.

Z. Radovan/www.BibleLandPictures.com

REFLECTION: Those who minister in the Lord's house, or temple, are the priests, for only the priests of the tribe of Levi could enter the temple. With few observers, and at night (v. 1), it would be easy to become complacent in carrying out one's duties. That is a temptation abundantly present in many opportunities of church service today. This psalm calls us to a proper attitude of worship in the performance of service to God.

Psalm 135

Carl Friedrich Heinrich Werner (1808–94)/
Private Collection/The Bridgeman Art Library

THEME: Praise the Lord who presides over heaven and has chosen and redeemed his people Israel.

TYPE: Hymn of praise/thanksgiving.

AUTHOR: Unknown.

BACKGROUND: God took Israel as his "treasured possession" in Exodus 19:5. This designation recurs here (v. 4) and in Deuteronomy 7:6; 14:2; 26:18; and Malachi 3:17. The exodus narratives of Exodus 1–18 regularly say that God did mighty acts so that they—be it Israel, Pharaoh, or the nations—would know that the Lord is God. Psalm 135 praises the name of the Lord and exalts him as greater than all "gods."

STRUCTURE: Stanza 1 (vv. 1–3) is a call to praise, which is followed by praise statements about the extent of God's rule in stanza 2 (vv. 4–7). Stanza 3 (vv. 8–14) continues with praise, now for God's actions in the exodus and conquest and his lasting reputation. Stanza 4 (vv. 15–18) is instruction about the powerlessness of idols and their followers. By contrast to the previous lines about the Lord's acts, they also serve to magnify the praise of the Lord. Stanza 5 (vv. 19–21) is another call to praise plus a final line of praise from the community.

SPECIAL NOTES: Psalm 136 is similar in that it first praises God for his acts of creation and then for the exodus and conquest.

Psalm 135:1 is similar to Psalm 113:1. Psalm 135:10–12 is similar to Psalm 136:17–22. Psalm 135:14 is the same as the beginning of Deuteronomy 32:36. Psalm 135:15–20 is similar to Psalm 115:4–11 (see also Isa. 44:6–20).

REFLECTION: "There is no God apart from me," says the Lord in Isaiah 45:21. Monotheism is not simply the belief that there is only one God and not many. It also means that there is no power beyond or outside of God. God has all power. No being can tap some power that is beyond God's control and use it against him. There is no such thing as "magic." But God has power to do as he wills. He created nature and can act supernaturally. When he delivered Israel from Egypt, there were no gods with any power to oppose him. And there still are none today. Believing in idols does not mean that they can do anything. The ideas of the world around Israel may have seemed common and powerful, but they were empty. How easy it is for us to see this truth when it comes to worshiping blocks of wood or metal. How much harder it is to realize the emptiness of the false worldviews around us. But the Word of the Lord stands forever. Have no doubts. "Praise him, you servants of the LORD."

Psalm 136

THEME: Praise the Lord, the Creator, who delivered and established Israel, for his love endures forever.

TYPE: Hymn of thanksgiving.

AUTHOR: Unknown.

PhotoDisc

STRUCTURE: The most obvious structural element in this psalm is that all the lines are two-part lines (bicola) that end with "His love endures forever." This structure suggests an antiphonal reading, where perhaps the assembled community gives the second half of each line as a response.

Four lines calling for praise to the Lord frame the psalm, three at the beginning and one at the end. In between are twenty-two lines of praise, giving the psalm a total of twenty-six lines. Stanza 1 (vv. 1–3) is a call to praise. Stanza 2 (vv. 4–9) praises God for his acts of creation. Stanzas 3 and 4 (vv. 10–22; v. 16 is a transition and might go with either stanza) praise God for his work in the exodus from Egypt and conquest of the Promised Land. At thirteen lines, these two stanzas praising God for his historical acts amount to exactly half of the psalm. Stanza 5 (vv. 23–25) praises God as a summary of the previous acts.

SPECIAL NOTES: Inside the frame, the psalm has exactly twenty-two lines of praise, the same as the number of letters in the Hebrew alphabet. This line count has been chosen for several psalms.

Psalm 135 is similar in that it first praises God for his power over creation and then the exodus and conquest.

REFLECTION: In Exodus 34:6 God declares his name to Moses: "The Lord, the compassionate and gracious God, slow to anger, abounding in love and faithfulness." This is one of the most fundamental affirmations about God in the Bible (cf. 2 Chron. 30:9; Neh. 9:17, 31; Pss. 86:15; 103:8; 111:4; 112:4; 145:8; Joel 2:13; and Jonah 4:2). From these traits, Psalm 136 lifts up God's abounding and enduring love. It is as enduring as creation, as personally and nationally significant as the redemption of Exodus, far outlasting the affirmation that echoes in our ears following twenty-six shouts that "his love endures forever." Bask in it.

Psalm 137

THEME: Though we cannot sing a Zion song for our captors, we cannot forget Zion.

TYPE: Communal lament.

AUTHOR: Unknown.

BACKGROUND: Nebuchadnezzar of Babylon destroyed Jerusalem in an attack of 587/6 BC and subsequently took the majority of the kingdom of Judah into exile (2 Kings 25). As a reprisal for rebelling against Babylon, the attack was brutal for those who resisted. The country of Edom aided in ransacking and pillaging Jerusalem. The short book of Obadiah is a prophetic oracle against Edom for its ravaging and plundering. Punishment oracles are leveled against Babylon as well in Isaiah 13 and 14; Jeremiah 50 and 51; and Habakkuk 2.

STRUCTURE: There are three stanzas of four lines each in this psalm. Stanza 1 (vv. 1–3) describes the original setting and occasion for the lament. Their captors demand that they sing Zion songs. Stanza 2 (vv. 4–6) laments the impossibility of the demand and instead uses the rhetoric of cursing themselves should they fail to remember and prize Jerusalem while in captivity. Stanza 3 (vv. 7–9) includes two imprecations, requests for God to judge Edom and Babylon.

SPECIAL NOTES: The imprecations in the final stanza, especially the one against Babylon, may sound disturbing at the initial reading. Several factors should be borne in mind. (1) Imprecations are primarily calls for judicial penalties to be applied to the guilty. (2) In the ancient world, punishment was thought of in ways that corresponded to the crime; for example, restitution plus fines for theft, or matching damages where restitution was not possible (not in terms of having restricted freedoms while serving jail time, which might be looked at as receiving free room and board). (3) Prophetic oracles have already been issued; that is, God has already decreed the punishments that match the crimes against Israel. So here the psalmist is asking for the prophecies to be fulfilled. (4) Given the character of warfare in the ancient Near East, it would not be unusual for the eventual downfall of a marauding kingdom to include such brutal acts. From the perspective of the human world, even the judgment oracles have a significant element of simply asserting that Babylon's own acts would come back to haunt it. What goes around comes around.

Todd Bolen/www.BiblePlaces.com

REFLECTION: Sometimes what used to bring joy brings pain. For example, when the traditional place for the family vacation becomes the place of a tragic family accident, the memories of the sad are intermingled with the happy. The potency of some tragedies short-circuits some of our ability to feel normal joys. This psalm comes from the juncture of such conflict. The songs are of strength and joy, but the setting mocks those things. What to do? This psalm says we must determine to remember the source of joy—here Zion—and the theology of God's strength and deliverance. And we must give to God our need to remember the tragedy and injustice.

Psalm 138

THEME: David said that regardless of what others around him did, he would praise the Lord, confident of his deliverance.

TYPE: Hymn of thanksgiving.

AUTHOR: Of David.

BACKGROUND: The psalmist is determined to bow toward the Lord's temple and praise him even when in front of idols. So this psalm was probably written for a time in Israel when idolatry was prevalent or for a setting outside the land of Israel, such as diplomatic missions or the exile. Daniel, for example, knelt to pray facing Jerusalem (Dan. 6:10). Since the psalm mentions the temple, rather than Jerusalem, it was probably for exiles before the destruction of the temple in 586 BC or after the temple was rebuilt in 515 BC.

STRUCTURE: The number of lines in the three stanzas makes a symmetrical pattern: 4-2-4. In stanza 1 (vv. 1–3) the psalmist announces the determination to praise the Lord in opposition to other options. Stanza 2 (vv. 4–5) is a call to praise that asserts the Lord's authority over all kingdoms. Stanza 3 (vv. 6–8) is a statement of confidence that God acts on behalf of the humble and will deliver the psalmist.

REFLECTION: Praising the true and living God in the presence of the "gods" and those who serve them shows boldness in enemy territory—like Daniel praying toward Jerusalem (cf. Ps. 138:2; Dan. 6:10) or his three friends not bowing before Nebuchadnezzar's idol (Dan. 3:8–18). But this is not the boldness of pride; it is the boldness of being humble before a mighty God. Submitting to whatever the crowd does or thinks to find acceptance is not commendable humility. But being humble before God, with a focused dependence on him, brings a boldness to stay true.

Psalm 139

THEME: The Lord has examined the psalmist and has complete knowledge of him; he sees the psalmist's longing for God to act against their common enemies.

TYPE: Mixed: Praise, lament, possibly royal.

AUTHOR: A psalm (*mizmor*) of David. For the director of music.

BACKGROUND: Though one of the more popular psalms to reflect on, its background is not certain. The beginning claim and the ending invitation for the Lord to test the psalmist imply a setting in which the psalmist wishes to assert his innocence. It has been suggested that the psalmist has been accused and this is part of his claim of innocence, or that these are the affirming words of the king as part of a larger ceremony. A lengthy praise section before a petition for protection from enemies is more typical of a communal lament, while this psalm is written in the singular. Together with the Davidic superscription, this may support the view that it is a royal psalm.

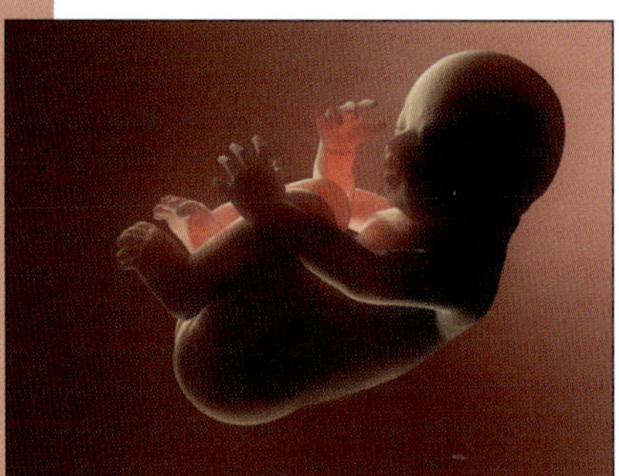

STRUCTURE: Stanza 1 (vv. 1–6) claims that the Lord has examined and known the psalmist with exhaustive knowledge. To demonstrate the extent of the Lord's awareness, stanza 2 (vv. 7–12) begins with a rhetorical question that the remainder of the stanza answers. God is aware of everywhere and can perceive the psalmist whether it is light or dark. Stanza 3 (vv. 13–18) expresses awe of God's design and work in fashioning the unborn baby. Given that God's knowledge is so vast and comprehensive, stanza 4 (vv. 19–24) asks why God does not attend to and slay the wicked. The psalmist also asks to be reexamined by God to be sure that there is no obstacle in his life that is a hindrance.

SPECIAL NOTES: Verses 15–16 are especially difficult, and the exact meaning of the "days" and the "book" is uncertain. Likely, the "days" refer to the time of embryonic development only. But if the speaker is the king, they might possibly refer also to his reign.

REFLECTION: The psalmist is both confident in and frustrated by God's ability to know and test him. The psalm is somewhat similar to Job 23, though partly it sounds opposite. Wanting to be vindicated, Job does not feel he can get a hearing and asserts that God is "not there" (Job 23:8) no matter which direction he turns. At the same time, he is sure that God knows his way. The psalmist says he cannot go anywhere without God knowing. So then, if God knows the psalmist so well, doesn't he also know everyone else as well? Why then doesn't he slay the wicked? The praise of God's intimate and encompassing knowledge is a frustration for understanding why God's enemies may act wickedly and misuse his name. In the end, we must also submit such inner conflict to the Lord, inviting him to search us and lead us in the way everlasting (vv. 23–24).

Psalm 140

© Brasil2/www.istockphoto.com

THEME: While scheming liars attack, the psalmist turns confidently to God and requests that the enemies' plots overtake them.

TYPE: Individual lament.

AUTHOR: A psalm (*mizmor*) of David. For the director of music.

BACKGROUND: The psalmist's opponents scheme, try to trap, and speak spitefully. This suggests that David is dealing with false accusations and possibly political plots against his leadership.

STRUCTURE: This psalm has four stanzas with three lines followed by a fifth stanza with two lines. Stanza 1 (vv. 1–3) is a petition for protection from poison-tongued attackers. Stanza 2 (vv. 4–5) matches stanza 1 in structure, beginning with a petition for protection followed by characterizations of the opponents' attacks. Stanza 3 (vv. 6–8) is a statement of confidence with a petition. Stanza 4 (vv. 9–11) continues to request, but is now imprecatory, asking for fitting justice against the opponents. Stanza 5 (vv. 12–13) concludes with a statement of confidence that God will act.

REFLECTION: "Rescue me," the psalmist cries, coupling his cry with an imprecation against those with the "poison of vipers on their lips." Using similarly strong imprecatory language, Jesus repeatedly denounces unrighteous religious leaders in Matthew 23; he even (like Isaiah, Jeremiah, John the Baptist, and Paul) echoes the metaphor of vipers (v. 23). The significance of the viper metaphor coils around their tendency to nest in cool, moist oases where weary travelers would expect refuge and rest. In addition, a "brood of vipers" usually refers to unrighteous and abusive leaders within the community of faith.

So when Jesus encourages us to pray, "Your kingdom come," what specifically might he be recommending? The psalmist's prayer here regarding "justice for the poor" and upholding "the cause of the needy" certainly seems likely. Perhaps Jesus is recommending the psalmist's strong imprecatory language as well: "may the mischief of their lips engulf them." This psalm, then, would serve as an expansion of the prayer, "Your kingdom come, your will be done, on earth as it is in heaven" (Matt. 6:10).

Psalm 141

© Paul Harris/www.awl-images.com

TYPE: Individual lament.

AUTHOR: A psalm (*mizmor*) of David.

BACKGROUND: The setting is the temple or tabernacle. Perhaps the psalmist comes to make a sin offering. Though there is no confession of sin, the petition suggests the psalmist is concerned about a personal weakness of joining with the wrong crowd in words and deeds.

STRUCTURE: Stanza 1 (vv. 1–2) is an initial appeal to be heard. The psalmist asks that his prayer would be accepted like the incense and sacrifices offered at the temple. In stanza 2 (vv. 3–4) he asks God to keep him from giving in to pressures to do wrong in word or deed. In stanza 3 (v. 5) he invites a personal rebuke to help prevent his acting in error, and in stanza 4 (vv. 6–7) he requests judgment against the wicked. In the last stanza (vv. 8–10) he combines a statement of loyalty, another petition to be protected from the traps that lead to evil, and a petition that the wicked be caught in their own traps.

THEME: The psalmist prays for protection against the pressure to join with the wrong crowd and also asks that their evil be made evident by their being caught in their own traps.

SPECIAL NOTES: The "lifting up of my hands" (v. 2) is another way of referring to praying, since raising the hands and face toward heaven was a common posture for prayer.

Verse 3 is reminiscent of Psalm 39:1.

REFLECTION: Blessed is the person who knows he or she needs accountability. How profitable it is to receive a rebuke. Proverbs 17:10 tells us that "a rebuke impresses a discerning person more than a hundred lashes a fool." And Ecclesiastes 7:5 tells us that "it is better to heed the rebuke of a wise person than to listen to the song of fools." The psalmist sets a model of not going it alone, but relying on others, to the point of welcoming a rebuke if needed.

Psalm 142

THEME: Lacking any refuge with people, the psalmist makes a complaint to God, seeking to be rescued.

TYPE: Individual lament.

AUTHOR: A *maskil* of David. A Prayer. When he was in the cave.

BACKGROUND: Psalm 57 includes a similar historical note. David hid from Saul in a cave with his men in 1 Samuel 24. In that account David bypassed an opportunity to assassinate Saul, and then Saul relented.

STRUCTURE: In stanza 1 (vv. 1–2) the psalmist addresses his companions, asserting his determination to take his troubles to the Lord. He then addresses the Lord in stanza 2 (vv. 3–4), first stating confidence in the Lord's care and then describing his perilous situation and lack of help. Stanza 3 (v. 5) is a statement of confidence and loyalty addressed to the Lord. The psalm closes with a petition to be rescued so that God will be praised.

SPECIAL NOTES: The term *maskil* in the title may mean either "skillful," which would be a reference to musical performance, or "making prudent," which would invite the reader to contemplation.

"My portion" (v. 5). The portion of each tribe was its allotment of land, from which it derived its sustenance. But the tribe of Levi received no allotment of land because of its responsibility to maintain the place of worship, oversee sacrifices, and perform other religious duties. As their portion the Levites received support from the other tribes (Num. 18:6–24; Deut. 18:1; Josh. 18:7) as well as the closeness to God that went with serving at the tabernacle or temple. Compare Psalms 16:5; 73:26; 119:57.

© SassyStock

REFLECTION: A path, a snare, a prison. My right hand, my refuge, my portion. These metaphors—figurative language without specific information, general enough to apply to all our lives—illustrate in this psalm the function and place of lament. Crying aloud, lifting our voice to tell God our troubles in loneliness and abandonment, confident that he is watching, we cry, "Rescue me, set me free." We can ask for his help, not because we are better than most, but because he is good, and in our asking for help, we bring praise to him.

Psalm 143

© Peter Chapman/www.BigStockPhoto.com

AUTHOR: A psalm (*mizmor*) of David.

STRUCTURE: A call for God to hear and answer begins each of two sections of seven lines.

Stanza 1 (vv. 1–2) is a call for God to listen and answer justly in the matter at hand, though not to put the psalmist on trial for justice. The psalmist does not claim complete innocence. Stanza 2 (vv. 3–4) makes accusations against the enemies whose pursuit has brought dismay. Stanza 3 (vv. 5–6) is a statement of loyalty and confidence expressed as turning to God. Stanza 4 (v. 7) is another call for the Lord to answer and protect from grave danger. Stanzas 5 and 6 (vv. 8–9 and 10) petition God for deliverance and guidance. Stanza 7 (vv. 11–12) closes the psalm with a petition for deliverance and punishment of the psalmist's enemies.

THEME: The psalmist prays that the Lord might rescue him from his enemies and lead him in God's ways.

TYPE: Individual lament.

REFLECTION: The psalmist seems to want both justice and mercy: judgment on the enemy and mercy for self. Is this a double standard? No, they are not in conflict here. The one who sings this psalm acknowledges the failure of all people, including himself or herself, and thus does not desire a comprehensive and absolute justice. That acknowledgment comes with a teachable spirit and desire to follow the Lord (v. 10). The basis for the appeal is not "how good I am," but God's name and his own righteousness (vv. 11, 1) and love (v. 12). The enemy is a destroyer, opposing the Lord's servant without mercy. Destruction of the unrepentant destroyer is mercy to the acknowledged teachable sinner. Justice and mercy are not in conflict, and the appeal for each depends on the different attitudes of the heart.

Psalm 144

THEME: Praise God for his aid; may he come with power against the enemy and bless the people.

TYPE: Royal.

AUTHOR: Of David.

BACKGROUND: This psalm specifically mentions God's servant David. God's victories through David are remembered to speak confidence into a new situation. The psalm was possibly used by any of David's descendants prior to going into battle. After the destruction of Jerusalem, it would express the community's desire for restoration and blessing.

Jay King

STRUCTURE: In stanza 1 (vv. 1–2) the king credits God as his aid and protector in battle. It is perhaps the community or its representative who recites stanza 2 (vv. 3–4). It sounds a note of humility, marveling at how God watches over human beings, as small and transient as they are. With the powerful imagery of a storm, the king petitions God to come down from heaven and rescue him from the power of lying foreigners in stanza 3 (vv. 5–8). In stanza 4 (vv. 9–10) the psalmist promises to praise God, the one who gives victory. Stanza 5 (v. 11) is another petition for deliverance from the false speakers. Stanza 6 (vv. 12–15) appears to be spoken by the community again, looking forward to the blessing of the requested deliverance.

SPECIAL NOTES: The false speech of the enemies may relate to the foreigners' breaking of a treaty, their assertion of false gods, denial of the Lord's sovereignty, or challenge of the Lord's anointed (cf. Ps. 2).

Stanza 2 is reminiscent of Psalm 8:4.

Stanzas 1 and 3 are reminiscent of Psalm 18:2 and 7–19.

REFLECTION: National protection and blessing are the two main themes of this psalm and are two of the chief ways by which the Lord makes his name known to the nations in the Old Testament (cf. Pss. 67, 82, 97). In the theme of protection, we hear the king speak with confident dependence, not self-aggrandizement and boasting, an example for all leaders. Humanity is very small for a God larger than heaven to be concerned with (vv. 3–4), so how very "blessed is the people whose God is the LORD" (v. 15).

Psalm 145

© Gino Santa Maria/www.istockphoto.com

(cf. Ex. 34:6; 2 Chron. 30:9; Neh. 9:17, 31; Pss. 86:15; 103:8; 111:4; 112:4; 145:8; Joel 2:13; and Jonah 4:2).

Stanza 1 (vv. 1–2) is a declaration of intent to praise the Lord forever. Stanza 2 (vv. 3–7) praises God, emphasizing the greatness of his deeds and how they span the generations. The wording of stanza 3 (v. 8) reaches back to Exodus 34:6, where God described his patient and compassionate character after Moses broke the tablets of the Ten Commandments in response to Israel's rebellious worship of the golden calf. Stanza 4 (vv. 9–13) praises God for the compassion he extends to all creation, and all creation praises him along with his servants. Stanzas 5 and 6 (vv. 14–17 and 18–20) develop praise around the themes of God's faithfulness and care. The last line (v. 21) extends a call to all creatures to respond with praise.

THEME: The faithful and caring Lord should be lauded by all across the generations.

TYPE: Hymn of praise.

AUTHOR: Of David. A psalm of praise.

STRUCTURE: Since a single opening or closing line is not unusual, this highlights the single line at verse 8, which contains a fundamental statement of the Lord's character

SPECIAL NOTES: This psalm is an alphabetic acrostic, with each line beginning with a successive letter of the Hebrew alphabet.

The second half of verse 13 was long ago skipped in the copying process but has been restored from the ancient Greek translation (called the Septuagint) and from a Hebrew Psalms document in the Dead Sea Scrolls, the oldest Hebrew manuscripts of the Bible. It is the *N* verse, "The LORD is trustworthy in all he promises and faithful in all he does."

REFLECTION: An alphabetic acrostic seems a fitting way to describe the indescribable—the greatness of God. The king ascribes greatness to his King while antiphonal voices answer him, like a resounding "Yes and amen." This is a glimpse of the Revelation vision in which John heard "every creature in heaven and on earth and under the earth and on the sea, and all that is in them, saying, 'To him who sits on the throne and to the Lamb be praise and honor and glory and power, for ever and ever!'" (Rev. 5:13). This is followed by a resounding "Amen" and a great vision of worship. We can only imagine, wait—and worship.

Psalm 146

THEME: Trust in the Lord, who is faithful, just, and compassionate, rather than in human leaders.

TYPE: Mixed: hymn of praise, instruction.

AUTHOR: Unknown.

STRUCTURE: An opening and closing "Hallelujah" frame the psalm. After a rhetorical call to self to praise God, the psalmist declares his intent to praise the Lord always (v. 2). The first full stanza (vv. 3–6) instructs the people not to trust in human princes but in God the Creator. The next stanza (vv. 7–9) praises God for his justice and compassion, words still addressed to the community. A final line praises the Lord for his enduring reign from Zion.

SPECIAL NOTES: Verse 5 is reminiscent of Psalm 84:12; verse 7 is reminiscent of Psalm 76:9; and verse 9 is reminiscent of Psalm 68:5–6.

REFLECTION: As there is no other god and no other power, so there is not really any other help besides the Lord. Here God is contrasted not with false gods, idols who cannot see or speak or act, but with humanity, who can. Humans have more life than "gods" and exert power over each other. But they are mortal and come to nothing. People may do good things to help others, or they may not. Regardless of whether they do or do not, they pass away. Only God endures. There is one God; he has all power; and he is good. Sin has brought us all manner of pains, but God is faithfully good forever. He heals, restores, advocates, guards, and sustains. He opposes the wicked. Our God reigns.

Psalm 147

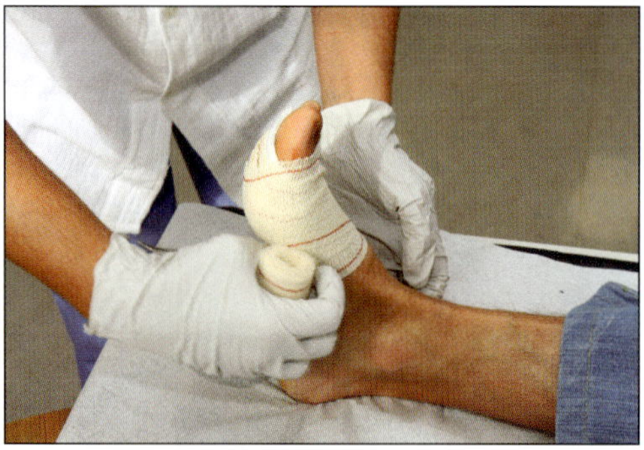

© Bojan Fatur/www.istockphoto.com

THEME: Praise the Lord, who rules nature and restores Jerusalem.

TYPE: Hymn of praise.

AUTHOR: Unknown.

BACKGROUND: Jerusalem and the temple were destroyed in Nebuchadnezzar of Babylon's attack of 587/586 BC. After Cyrus of Persia conquered Babylon in 539 BC, he allowed the Jews to return to the land of Israel and to return the articles from the temple taken by the Babylonians. The temple was rebuilt under the leadership of Haggai, Zechariah, and Zerubbabel. Later the wall of Jerusalem was rebuilt under the leadership of Nehemiah. Prior to the destruction of Jerusalem, there were many prophecies of their eventual return to the land. These are often called restoration oracles. This psalm celebrates the exiles' return and the rebuilding of Jerusalem.

STRUCTURE: An opening and closing "Hallelujah" frame the psalm. After an opening line extolling the virtue of praising the Lord, the line pattern of the stanzas demonstrates symmetry: 1-2-7-2-7-2.

The three sets of two lines discuss God's dealings with Israel. In verses 2–3 he brings the exiles back to Jerusalem and heals them. In verses 10–11 the Lord favors those who fear him rather than cavalry or infantry. In verses 19–20 he has given his word and laws to Israel and none other.

Verses 4–9 and 12–18 each have seven lines in the Hebrew text. Verses 4–9 praise God primarily as he directs and controls creation. The center line (v. 7) is a call to praise, dividing the group into two sections. Verses 12–18 begin with a call to praise and praise God for strengthening Jerusalem and his direction of the weather. The center line (v. 15) extols his authority through his commanding word, dividing the group into two sections. The psalm has many inner connections between its various parts, so that the last two lines (vv. 19–20) sound like a continuation of 2–3 and 10–11 or a continuation of 13–14.

SPECIAL NOTES: Compare verses 10–11 with Psalm 33:16–18.

REFLECTION: In 1822 John Howard Payne penned the famous lines "Mid pleasures and palaces though we may roam, be it ever so humble, there's no place like home!" Imagine the exile, being forced by Babylon to relocate outside Judah and Israel for many long, hard years. Then imagine the promised return. Feelings were no doubt mixed as the place held many memories, and the results of past destruction were still evident. We may have to wait for God's timing, but "he heals the brokenhearted and binds up their wounds" (Ps. 147:3).

Psalm 148

THEME: All heaven and earth should praise the Lord their Creator, who has exalted Israel.

TYPE: Hymn of praise.

AUTHOR: Unknown.

STRUCTURE: An opening and closing "Hallelujah" frame the psalm. Stanza 1 (vv. 1–4) is a call to praise addressed to the angels and parts of creation in the heavens. Stanza 2 (vv. 5–6) is a summary call to praise plus praise for God as their Creator. Stanza 3 (vv. 7–12) is a call to praise addressed to the earthly creation, creatures, and all people. Stanza 4 (vv. 13–14) is a summary call to praise (first repeating v. 5) plus praise that God is exalted over heaven and earth and has exalted his people Israel.

SPECIAL NOTES: *Horn* (v. 14). This imagery of the horn comes from bulls (not the ram's horn used as a trumpet) and possibly from two bulls fighting each other with their horns. So the horn of the wicked or of the righteous symbolizes their strength or victory. Compare Psalms 18:2; 22:21; 75:4–5, 10; 89:17; 92:10; 112:9.

Psalms 148–150 use various lists in their calls to praise. Psalm 148 calls all of heaven and earth and all people to praise the Lord. Psalm 149 calls Israel to praise the Lord. Psalm 150 calls all to praise the Lord with musical instruments.

REFLECTION: There is a time for a solo—an individual hymn of thanksgiving, but this is an occasion to join the magnificent choir of all creation and creatures. And God's worth is beyond them all. Nevertheless, his people are close to his heart. How marvelous the grace of such a glorious God!

Psalm 149

© Bold Stock

THEME: Let Israel praise the Lord, who grants it victory over its enemies.

TYPE: Hymn of praise.

AUTHOR: Unknown.

BACKGROUND: This psalm was probably used in a ceremony before the king led his people to battle from Jerusalem.

STRUCTURE: An opening and closing "Hallelujah" frame the psalm. After a one-line call to sing (v. 1), there are two stanzas of four lines each. Stanza 1 (vv. 2–5) calls God's people to praise him and affirms that he is pleased with them and gives them victory. Stanza 2 expands on that thought from verse 4. Verses 6–9 ask that God's praise be in the mouths of soldiers equipped for war, to execute judgment on the peoples as it has been written (perhaps prophesied or otherwise ordained by God).

SPECIAL NOTES: Psalms 148–150 use various lists in their calls to praise. Psalm 148 calls all of heaven and earth and all people to praise the Lord. Psalm 149 calls Israel to praise the Lord. Psalm 150 calls all to praise the Lord with musical instruments.

REFLECTION: Calling for praise to the King, this psalm continues the buildup to the finale. It calls the warriors to wield their swords, to stand at attention, ready for the battle to which they are called. Rich with imagery, this psalm can also be a call for us today. We are called to stand for righteousness and justice with our King, who intercedes for the helpless and the persecuted. We stand with him and for his kingdom when we help the least of his followers and when we pray, "Your kingdom come, your will be done." Let us so stand and offer our bodies as living sacrifices.

Psalm 150

THEME: Praise the Lord for his mighty deeds with all manner of musical instruments.

TYPE: Hymn of praise.

AUTHOR: Unknown.

STRUCTURE: An opening and closing "Hallelujah" frame the psalm. The intervening lines call all to praise the Lord (for his deeds, which could be understood in light of the victories of Ps. 149), making use of many musical instruments.

SPECIAL NOTES: Psalms 148–150 use various lists in their calls to praise. Psalm 148 calls all of heaven and earth and all people to praise the Lord. Psalm 149 mentions two musical instruments in its call to Israel to praise the Lord (who gives victory over the peoples). Psalm 150 calls all to praise the Lord with musical instruments.

Designpics

REFLECTION: This is the finale. The Psalter began with a word to the wise about the value of being rooted in Scripture. It compiled many laments and hymns of praise. It intersected with the role of the king and the place of Zion. It advised our worldview. The final psalms are hymns of praise recognizing God's sovereignty over all and inviting all to praise him. It ends with great fanfare. Indeed, "let everything that has breath praise the LORD" (v. 6).

Share Your Thoughts

With the Author: Your comments will be forwarded to the author when you send them to *zauthor@zondervan.com.*

With Zondervan: Submit your review of this book by writing to *zreview@zondervan.com.*

Free Online Resources at

www.zondervan.com

Zondervan AuthorTracker: Be notified whenever your favorite authors publish new books, go on tour, or post an update about what's happening in their lives at www.zondervan.com/authortracker.

Daily Bible Verses and Devotions: Enrich your life with daily Bible verses or devotions that help you start every morning focused on God. Visit www.zondervan.com/newsletters.

Free Email Publications: Sign up for newsletters on Christian living, academic resources, church ministry, fiction, children's resources, and more. Visit www.zondervan.com/newsletters.

Zondervan Bible Search: Find and compare Bible passages in a variety of translations at www.zondervanbiblesearch.com.

Other Benefits: Register yourself to receive online benefits like coupons and special offers, or to participate in research.